Follow the Money

I0489984

Copyright © 2018 by Butch Robinson Jr

Published by: CreateSpace Independent
Publishing Platform

ISBN:13:9781720666387

ISBN-Printed in the USA

Case Brief

The following is a case about a homicide ordered by a well-known New York narcotics dealer named Bulldog who ran the north side of the Harlem cocaine industry. He was rumored to have ordered a hit on the man he believed to be interfering with his drug trade. Though this case developed into a RICO case (Racketeer Influenced and Corrupt Organizations Act) handled by the U.S. Attorney's office, Detective Tony Richards with the New York City Homicide Division was initially assigned to the investigation.

FOLLOW THE MONEY

Chapter 1

Detective Sergeant Sonia Richards poked her head into the bullpen area of the homicide office. "Who's up?" she yelled.

Sonia Richards had been a detective for almost two decades, and a sergeant for several years. Though people sometimes assumed they were related, it was just coincidence that she shared a last name with one of her detectives.

"I'm up," said Detective Tony Richards. "Whatchya got?"

"We've got a man down and out in the lobby of twenty-six thirty-eight Tremont Avenue. You and Detective Morris get ready to roll out and I'll meet you guys at the scene."

"Okay, Sergeant," Tony said as Detective Sergeant Richards headed in the other direction. "Meet you up there."

"I'll get the homicide kit," said Detective Van Morris. Tony and Van had been partners for a few years.

A few minutes later, Tony and Van were out the door and on their way to the scene of the homicide. By the time they arrived at 2638 Tremont Avenue, a small crowd had gathered in front of the building. Both civilians and law enforcement were present, creating a low din as they muttered amongst themselves about the crime that had just occurred. Officers Williams and Robinson had stationed themselves just inside the lobby to keep nosy onlookers at bay and safeguard the crime scene.

"Tony," Van said, "we got a lot of possible witnesses out here. We may need to get some suits over here - this is a big building and a small crowd." "Good idea, Van. I'll notify central while you get the kit." Van nodded and headed toward the apartment building. Tony spoke into his radio. "Homicide squad to central. Kay," he said, signaling the end of his transmission.

"Homicide squad, go with your message. Kay."

"We need several additional units to respond to twenty-six thirty-eight Tremont Avenue for crowd control. No emergency. Kay."

"Ten four. Additional units, no emergency. Kay."

"Ten four," Tony replied. He started walking toward the building, shouting across the mass of onlookers that had gathered. "May I have your attention, please? This is a homicide and we would like your help." He continued to address the crowd as he walked. "Please don't leave until you have spoken to the police, whether you saw anything or not. I repeat, please stand fast until you have spoken with the police. Thank you for your cooperation." He gave a slight wave of his right hand as he entered the lobby and joined Van just inside.

"Detectives," Officer Robinson said with a nod of his head, greeting Tony and Van as his partner, Officer Williams, joined the trio.

"What's up, guys?" Van said in response.

"Who's writing?" asked Tony.

"I'm recording," confirmed Officer Robinson.

"Okay," Tony replied. "Whatchya got?"

"Me and my partner got shots fired at approximately thirteen fifteen hours. We responded immediately," Officer Robinson began. "When we arrived, a small group of people were standing out front, all saying a man was dead inside the lobby. We approached the lobby with weapons drawn and found the victim lying on the floor in a pool of blood. Officer Williams called central and asked for a bus, detectives, and a patrol supervisor. Sergeant

Vara showed up soon after and took the wife of the victim to the house."

"The wife of the victim?" Tony interrupted, looking at Officer Williams.

"Yeah," answered Officer Williams. "Said she saw the shooting."

"Alright, thanks," said Tony. "Robinson, do a DD5 for me when you get back to the house." Officer Robinson nodded and agreed to complete the paperwork back at the office. As he and Officer Williams walked off, an Emergency Medical Services officer came over.

"Who's catching?" asked the EMS officer.

"I am," answered Tony. "Time of death is thirteen twenty-eight hours. EMS eight three six Rogers."

"Tony Richards, one two three homicide squad."

"Take care guys."

"You as well."

Detective Sergeant Richards showed up with two other detectives. "Whatchya got, Tony?" his boss asked.

"Right now, male shot in the head numerous times. His wife, who's a possible witness, saw the shooting and was escorted over to the house by Sergeant Vara"

"The wife's at the house now?"

"Yeah, that's what I've been told."

"Okay, well, you take charge here and I'll go back to the house and sit on the witness," she said, motioning to the two beside her. "We have two new detectives who are joining our team. You should know Detective Dee Ragland and Detective Kay Bradberry. They worked the midnight squad and just switched to the day squad."

Tony extended his hand and said, "Yeah, we know these guys pretty well."

Smiling in agreement, Van also extended his hand. "Yeah," he said, winking. "They're collar thieves. Don't leave any wanted cards around when they're working."

In response to the ribbing, Detective Bradberry said, "You got that right. I'll steal the shirt right off your back." She shook the hands of both men before Detective Ragland stepped forward to do the same.

"Detective Richards. Detective Morris," said Detective Ragland, nodding at each man respectively. With a mischievous smirk he added, "This is gonna be great working alongside legends like you two."

"Legends in our own minds, maybe," Tony kidded good-naturedly. "But seriously, Dee and Kay, it's good to have great detectives like you working with us."

Assistant District Attorney Robbie Ross showed up just then. "Well, what have we got here? A family reunion?" he teased, laughing out loud. He nodded towards the victim and said, "I think I know everybody here except the guy kissing the ground over there. How's everyone doing?"

The five of them had worked together on a homicide a few years back, and they spent a minute or so talking about what they had each been up to since then. "Okay," Ross began, as they quickly refocused on the current crime scene. "I've got my man, Ramy, to video the scene, if that's alright."

"No problem," Tony said as the videographer walked up. "Ramy! How you been?"

"I'm doing fine. How are you detectives doing?" Ramy replied, reaching out to shake the hands of everyone in the group. "It shouldn't take that long to video the area. You guys are still waiting on the M.E. to arrive, right?"

"Yeah," Van responded, looking over his shoulder for the medical examiner. "Soon as he gets here, we'll be able to move along with this investigation."

Ramy left the group, but returned just five minutes later. "I'm all done," he said.

"Great," said Ross. "I'll pick that video up at the office when you're done."

"You got it," Ramy answered. "Well, detectives, good luck in finding the perp. I'll catch you guys later."

"Take care, Ramy. Thanks, man," Tony said as Ramy saluted them and walked away.

Tony asked the other detectives to go back outside to collect names and canvass for him while he waited on the medical examiner to respond, and Detectives Ragland and Bradberry left to conduct interviews. While waiting for the medical examiner to arrive, Tony, Van, and ADA Robbie Ross speculated about the murder. About ten minutes later, Mr. West arrived.

"What's up, guys?" he greeted the men. "Who's catching?"

"I am," Tony replied.

"What's your shield?" Mr. West asked.

"It's one two three."

"Got it."

"You got a pair of gloves?" Van asked him.

"Yeah," he said, smirking at Van's rhetorical question. "I do."

"Then glove up!" Tony added. "Let's get this done."

After following Tony's obvious instructions, the medical examiner started with the pockets of the victim. He removed a wallet and pulled out an ID. He held it up.

"License picture looks like the victim," he said. "We'll call him ID'd for now until we get a positive ID at the morgue with prints and dental. Name on the driver's license is Carl White. Date of birth is five, twenty-one, sixty-five. Address matches this location." West continued to search through the wallet. "He's got twenty dollars in US currency, social security card, Blockbuster card, and a registration card."

After identifying everything discovered in the victim's wallet, he moved on to assessing his wounds.

"Several wounds to the head," the medical examiner announced. "Looks like four shots, which appears to be the cause of death." As West continued to examine the body, Detective Ryan Riggs of the crime scene unit showed up.

"Hey, everybody," said Detective Riggs.

"What up?" Van replied.

"Hey, Riggs!" Tony chimed in.

The medical examiner was the last to greet Detective Riggs as he finished his examination. He stood up, removed his gloves, and nodded at him in acknowledgement of his arrival. "How are you?" West asked as Detective Riggs greeted him with a hearty pat on the back. "Just about finished here, so you can have the scene soon as I finish my schematic."

"Take your time, sir," Detective Riggs replied as Assistant District Attorney Ross rejoined the group, just ending a call on his cell phone.

"Hey, Ryan! What's going on, dude?" Ross asked.

"Not much. How you doin'?"

"I'm here," Ross replied with a grin.

Just then, the medical examiner clapped his hands once and rubbed them together. "Alright," West said. "He's all yours, detectives. And when you finish with the body, my pickup van is en route to pick up the victim. See you guys for the autopsy later."

"Thanks, Mr. West," Tony replied. "We'll see you later."

As the medical examiner left the scene, Detective Riggs took out his camera and began filming the area. He knelt down and placed plate cards near the four spent shells, then placed the ID into a crime scene evidence bag and handed it to Tony. He opened the brown paper bag next to the victim. Inside the bag was a hand gun: a .25 semi-automatic, silver with brown handles. There were also four tin foils of a white, powdery substance that looked like cocaine. Riggs put the gun and the foils into separate evidence bags and, consistent with the chain of custody requirements, he gave them to Tony as well.

"Detective Richards," Riggs said as he stood up. "You need anything else?"

"Just the prints if you find any on the weapon".

"Ten four," Riggs answered. "You guys take care and good luck with the investigation".

"Alright, then. I'll be leaving," Ross said. "Call me if you guys need anything."

"Thanks, man," said Tony, and Van said the same. Fifteen minutes later, the body wagon guys showed up with a stretcher and removed the body from the lobby so they could take him to the morgue.

"Alright, partner," Van said. "You ready to get to work on this one?"

"Let's do this," Tony replied.

They left the building and joined Detectives Ragland and Bradberry in interviewing the people standing around outside. Through their collective efforts, they had interviewed everyone after about thirty minutes.

"Here's where we're at," Tony started. "All the preliminary work has been done. What's left is the canvass of the building. It's sixteen floors, so we'll break it up." He pointed at Detectives Ragland and Bradberry. "Dee and Kay, you two take the top eight floors. Van and I have to leave to go interview the wife and then we'll come back and finish the building."

"You got it, boss," Detective Bradberry said, drawing her hand to her forehead in a mock salute to Tony.

"Hey, no salute needed. I'm a peon just like you," Tony answered. "Don't call me 'boss'."

"She's just kidding, *boss*," teased Detective Ragland.

Van joined in. "Yeah, boss," he said. "Lighten up, sir." They all started laughing.

"Alright, alright. Get to work or I'll write you all up," Tony said, still laughing, and they all went their separate ways to begin work on their respective assignments.

Chapter 2

Back at the homicide squad, Detective Sergeant Sonia Richards had been consoling the wife of the victim. She had gotten her something to eat, and had another female officer taking care of her daughter for a bit. Though obviously shaken from the experience, they were doing as well as could be expected. When Tony and Van arrived, they immediately introduced themselves to the victim's wife.

"Hello, Ms. White, is it?" Tony asked.

"Lashay. Alicia Lashay," she replied. "Carl and I never officially got married."

"Sorry," Tony replied. "I just assumed you were of the same last name. Ms. Lashay, my partner and I would like to offer you our condolences about your husband. My name is Detective Richards and this is Detective Morris." Van nodded and smiled at the woman. "We would also like to interview you about what occurred to cause his death. Were you present when this happened?"

"Yeah, I was there when that man shot my husband."

"Did you see anything?" Van asked.

"I didn't see his face but I remember what he was wearing."

"Okay," Tony said. "How about you start from the beginning and tell us what happened, step by step, after you left your apartment?" Alicia agreed.

"Me and Carl and Tanya – my fifteen-month-old baby girl – got on the elevator."

"What apartment did you come from?" Van interjected.

"Fourteen E," Alicia answered. "We got on the elevator – Carl was carrying the garbage because it wouldn't go down the garbage chute. So, we got on the elevator and pressed the lobby button, but it stopped on the eighth floor and a small Hispanic lady got on with us. When we got to the lobby, I got off first with Tanya and Carl following behind me.

"Then I saw this guy with a black hooded sweatshirt and jeans just standing behind this pillar with his hood on. I remember thinking it was weird, but I kept walking. Then I heard this *bang, bang, bang, bang* It was four times and it was real loud. I looked back and saw that same guy holding a gun and my husband falling to the ground. I got so scared. I thought he was going to kill all of us, so I started to run out of the building." Her voice trailed off as she put her head in her hands. She looked back up at the two detectives. "I forgot about my daughter," she added and then started crying.

Tony handed her a tissue and consoled her by rubbing her shoulder. "It's alright," Tony told her. "There was nothing you could have done to stop him from killing your husband."

"Thanks," Alicia said, halfheartedly, before continuing with her story. "I ran outside and the lady who was in the elevator – I don't even know her name – she grabbed my daughter and ran outside with me."

"Did you get a look at his face when you saw him holding the gun?" Van asked.

"No," she answered. "He was a black guy, but I didn't really see his face".

"You may remember more about him if you close your eyes," Van said. "Try this for me. Close your eyes and go back to that moment. Try to picture the face of the person who killed your husband. Start with his eyes." Alicia followed Van's instructions and closed her eyes. "You said he wore a hoodie," Van continued, "so you don't know if he has hair or not. But what color are his eyes? Think hard."

"Light," Alicia replied. "I remember he had really light eyes, like grey or green. Very light eyes."

"Good," Tony said, taking over. "Now are you sure about the hoodie and pants he was wearing? Do you remember the colors?"

"Definitely," Alicia confirmed. "Black hoodie, blue jeans."

"What about his shoes?" asked Tony.

"I don't know."

"How tall is he? Is he as tall as your husband or shorter?"

"He's a little shorter than my husband."

"Great. Do you know if you have ever seen him before?"

"No."

"Would you be able to recognize him if you saw him again?"

"Maybe if he had on a hood or something," Alicia said. "Yeah. I may be able to recognize him".

"You see," Van interjected. "I told you that you may know more than you think. Sometimes closing your eyes helps to bring some things back."

"What type of work did your husband do?" Tony asked.

"Well, he didn't have no real job," Alicia replied honestly. "He sold drugs for a living. He *was* working for a meat market cutting meats. But then he got this idea to sell coke from this guy at the butcher shop. He used to give this guy a good deal on meat and just charge him a couple dollars. Then outta nowhere one day, this guy just offered him some coke at a discounted price. It started from there."

"Where did he sell coke at?" asked Tony.

"Up in Harlem. 149th and Eighth. He would go sell from five to one, and then he'd come back home."

"Who'd he get the coke from?"

"I don't know. He never told me the guy's name and I never met him."

"Do you know why your husband got killed?"

"I got an idea," she answered. "Some guy was jealous. Told my husband not to sell drugs on the block no more. Carl said he told the guy he needed to make some money, but the guy told him this was his town and he owns the streets. Said Carl was taking money from his pockets. So, Carl told him that they could all eat, and there was enough to go around, but this guy didn't agree. He told Carl he had no business even eating his scraps on his streets, and that if he didn't stop selling in his areas, he would put a stop to it. But Carl didn't back down. Carl just told him to do what he had to do because he didn't plan to stop until he was ready to stop. I know that guy had Carl killed. I know it." She started to cry again and Tony handed her more tissues. She took them and wiped her nose.

"How do you know this guy was involved?" Van asked. "Has he contacted you?

"I guess I don't know for sure," she answered. "But I really think he had something to do with it. Got some other guy to kill him or something."

"Do you know this guy?" asked Tony, taking the box of tissues back from Alicia. "The guy who threatened Carl?"

"No. But I know they call him Bulldog," she offered. "He's supposed to be some big drug dealer. They say he owns the north side of Harlem. You don't know who Bulldog is?"

"No," Tony replied. "We mainly work in the Bronx, so we don't keep up with what happens in the other boroughs. Plus, we're not narcotics cops. But I'm sure the cops from that area know him. Do you know his real name?"

"No," she answered.

"Is there anything else that you can tell us about this Bulldog guy?" Van probed. "Where he lives? What type of car he drives? Anything else?"

Alicia shook her head. "Not too much. I just heard that he's real young, he lives in Sugar Hill, he drives a gold Benz, and he always rides around doing wheelies on a motorcycle."

Van widened his eyes and said, "I thought you didn't know this guy at all. But that's a lot of good information." Tony nodded in agreement.

"Well, I never thought about him before," Alicia started. "But I'm tellin' you, either he did it or he paid someone else to do it."

"Alright," Tony said. "Well, I'll just need to get some pedigree information on you if you don't mind."

"Pedigree?" she asked.

"Yeah," Tony answered. "Just a few identifying details about you."

"Go ahead," she replied. "I don't mind."

"Okay," Tony started, "what is your date of birth?"

"Seven. Twenty-two. Seventy-seven."

"Do you have a job?"

"Yeah. I'm a supermarket clerk at Pathmark."

"What are your hours at Pathmark?"

"Four-fifteen to eleven-fifteen, Monday through Friday. I'm off Saturday and Sunday."

"Who's on the family registry at housing?"

"We both are."

"How long had you been living there together?"

"About five years."

"Does Carl have any living relatives?"

"Yeah. His mom lives in Harlem. And his two sisters live there with her."

"What's her name and address?"

"Ann White," Alicia shared. "She lives at thirty-two twenty, Eighth Avenue, apartment four-A."

"Thanks. Any other relatives?"

"Just the sisters, Yazmin and Aleya White. They may know more about Bulldog than I do because they've lived up in Harlem their entire lives."

"Do you have any relatives living, Ms. Lashay?" Van asked.

"Just my mother, Amaryllis Lashay," Alicia replied. "She lives here in the Tilden projects."

"Is there anything else that you can give us to bring this investigation to a close?" asked Tony.

"Not that I can think of," she answered.

"Alrighty, then," Tony said. "Detective Morris and I are going to drive you home and continue to be in touch with you, if that's okay."

"That should be fine, Detective Richards."

"Anything else you can think of, Detective Morris?" Tony asked, looking at his partner.

"No," Van responded. "That should about cover it".

"Okay, then," Tony said, turning back to the victim's wife. "Give us a few minutes and we'll get your daughter and escort you back home."

"Alright," she said, and the two detectives left the interview room. They headed to the sergeant's office and found the door half open. They knocked on the door jam and were immediately waived inside.

"What's up, guys?" asked Detective Sergeant Sonia Richards as she hung up her desk phone.

"Hey, Sergeant," Tony said. "We have a start."

"I'm listening," she replied.

"The victim's wife says they entered the elevator with an older Hispanic lady they didn't know, and then noticed a suspicious black male wearing a black hoodie pulled over his head in the lobby," Tony began. "She heard four shots, and saw the guy in the black hoodie standing over her husband holding a gun. She says she can't I.D. the perp, except for having very light eyes. She didn't seem to know much, but thinks a black male from Harlem by the street-name of Bulldog is the one responsible for the murder. Says he runs coke in the north part of Harlem and had beef with her husband about territory. She doesn't know Bulldog but says he drives a gold Benz and does wheelies on a motorcycle up and down Eighth Avenue all the time. She thinks he's about twenty-two and lives in Sugar Hill. And that's where we're at."

Detective Sergeant Richards nodded. "Okay," she began. "So, we work this guy, Bulldog, and get all the information we can on him and see where that leads us. Has the canvass been done yet?"

"No. Dee and Kay are still canvassing," he told her. "We figured we'd drop off the wife and then join them to conduct the rest of the canvass."

"Sounds like a plan. Keep me posted," she said.

After leaving Detective Sergeant Richards' office, Tony and Van escorted Alicia Lashay and her child back to her apartment. Tony informed her that they would be in touch, gave her his card, and got her phone number. They met up with Detectives Ragland and Bradberry on the ninth floor.

"Dee, Kay," Van greeted them. "How y'all doin'?"

"What up," Detective Bradberry said. "We're almost done with this canvass. We've just got two more apartments to do."

"Anything good to tell us?" Tony asked.

"Nah. It's up too high," Detective Bradberry answered. "Most people just thought it was firecrackers."

"Alright," Tony replied. "Thanks. When you're done just type up the DD5s and leave them in the office."

"Did you guys get anything from the wife?" Detective Ragland asked.

"Actually, yes," said Tony. "She gave us a good bit of information, but we'll share that with you when we get back to the house. You know, just in case the walls have ears." He winked and gestured to the apartments all around.

"You're right," Detective Ragland said. "We'll see you at the house. Take care."

"We'll finish up downstairs. See ya," Van said, and Tony gave a brief wave of his hand. The two men walked down to the next floor and started their canvass. An hour later, they were done and headed back to the house to start their DD5s.

Chapter 3

When they arrived back at the house, all of the detectives immediately began working on their DD5s. About two hours after starting his paperwork, Tony received a phone call from an anonymous male who claimed to have information on Carl White's murder. The caller was hesitant about giving his name, but after some cajoling, agreed to meet the following day.

Tony and Van pulled into the parking lot at the house at the same time the next morning.

"What's this?" Tony shouted over the roof of his car at his usually tardy partner, making an exaggerated point to look at his watch. "A new trend?"

"You got a problem with self-improvement?" Van retorted. "I figured you'd be here early, so I decided to meet you here and get started right away."

Shaking his head and laughing, Tony said, "No problems here, partner. Let's go chart out a to-do list."

A few minutes later, Detective Sergeant Richards showed up in the office. "Who died that brought you two inside the office so early?" she asked, wide-eyed.

"It's the new me, Sergeant," Van answered. "I am going to be on time from now on. You watch and see."

"You know I don't actually think this will last too long, don't you?" she replied.

"Trust me, Sergeant. It will."

"Alright. We'll see," she said and went inside her office.

"We'll have to meet this guy named Greg in a half hour near Fox Street," Tony said to Van.

"After that, breakfast?" Van asked.

"If you're buying, Mr. Money Bags."

"Why I gotta buy?"

"'Cause you got the money, Mr. Money Bags."

"Fine. I'll buy," Van agreed, and they went to their respective desks to review some notes and organize some paperwork. Thirty minutes later, they told the sergeant that they were headed out to meet with and talk to a possible witness.

"Be careful, guys," she warned. "Make sure you pat him down before he gets inside the vehicle."

"Will do," Tony assured her, and he and Van left to drive over to Fox Street and 179th. When they spotted a man they believed to be the possible witness, they pulled up to the curb and got out of the car.

"Detectives," the man on the street greeted them.

"How ya doin'?" Tony replied. "You Greg?"

"Yeah, I'm Greg."

"My name is Detective Tony Richards, and this is my partner, Detective Van Morris. You said you have information about the homicide?"

"Yeah, I do," Greg said, shifting his eyes nervously.

"Alright, well, first we have to toss you to make sure you're not carrying any weapons," Tony explained. "Then we have to transport you over to the homicide squad. Is that alright with you?"

"That's cool," answered Greg. "I would be a fool to have a weapon on me if I'm meeting with detectives."

"You are correct," Van agreed. "But unfortunately, we meet some fools in our line of work. Put your hands against the car and spread open your legs." Van started patting Greg down, first checking his right side, starting with his wrist and moving down to his feet. He then did the same thing with his left side. After completing the search, Van told Greg to get in the back seat behind the passenger's seat, and he complied without hesitation. As soon as they got back to the house, they took Greg upstairs to the interview room.

Chapter 4

Both detectives entered the interview room and took seats.

"I have to get your pedigree information first," Tony started. "Then you can tell us whatever you know. Your full name?"

"Greg James."

"Your date of birth?"

"Eight. Eight. Seventy-five."

"Address?"

"I live at Tilden houses. Twenty-six thirty-five Tremont Avenue, apartment five-C."

"Phone number?"

"212-555-1357. That's my beeper. You can put in a code and I'll call you back."

"Do you live alone or with family?"

"I live with my mom and two little brothers."

"Alright, Greg," Tony said, leaning back in his chair and looking directly at the alleged witness. "Tell us what you know."

"I knew Carl," Greg started. "He was a decent guy. He did his thing, but not around the way.

Only sold coke up in Harlem. I heard he had a beef with Shorty, and then Shorty shot him."

"Who's Shorty?" Tony asked.

"Shorty's this other guy I know," Greg answered vaguely. "Sells marijuana around the way."

"And what is Shorty's real name?"

"Dave Wes."

"Do you know where Mr. Wes lives?"

"Nah. But I know where he pitches at."

"Where?"

"He sells bud by One Seventy-Fifth and Tremont. On the corner."

Van interjected then. "So, did you see Shorty shoot Carl?"

"No," Greg replied, and briefly looked down at his feet. He looked back up at Van. "But I heard he did. I heard they had an argument over the weed, and that Carl slapped him and told him he better get him his money. But I don't know how much Shorty owed him."

"So, this was about money?" Van asked, raising one eyebrow.

"That's what I heard," Greg replied and then randomly added, "and Shorty drives a white Honda."

Van furrowed his brow and sighed in frustration. "Okay, so you didn't see Shorty shoot Carl. Who did see it?"

"I don't know."

"So, who told you Shorty shot Carl?"

"Can't tell you that," Greg answered.

Getting more impatient, Van asked, "How are we gonna corroborate your story if you didn't see the shooting, and you don't know who saw the shooting, and you won't say who told you about the shooting?"

"Hey, I never said I knew someone who saw the shooting," Greg answered defensively.

"So, this is all just hearsay?" Van asked.

"Well, I just thought you guys might wanna know what's being said around the way," said Greg. "This way at least you have someone to look at, right?"

"Right," said Van, rubbing his forehead. "And I don't want you to get the wrong idea. We do appreciate your coming forward. But if you do hear of anyone who saw the shooting, it could financially benefit you. Now, I know money wouldn't be the motive for your help. You're just a decent person, and we do appreciate the fact that you're here helping us with this case."

"Anything else you have to add?" Tony asked.

"No," Greg answered, shaking his head. "That was it."

"Okay, then," Tony said, half-smiling and reaching across his desk. "Here. Take my card. And if you hear anything else, give us a call, alright?"

"Alright."

Tony stood up. "Detective Morris and I will drop you off right where we picked you up, if that's okay."

"Yeah, that would be fine."

"Van, you got anything else?"

"No, sir, Detective Richards," Van announced as he rose from his chair. "I'm ready. Let's ride."

All three men got up and left the office. They dropped Greg off and headed to the 161st Street Diner for breakfast. They found a seat at a booth in the back, and were happy to have a waiter come over to the table immediately.

"How you guys doin' today?" the waiter asked as he pulled a pen and a pad out of the black apron tied around his waist. "Can I get you something?"

"Yeah," Van said. "We'll take two cups of coffee for now with cream and sugar."

The waiter left the table and was back with the coffee just two minutes later. "You guys ready to order?"

"Yeah," Tony started. "I'll take three pancakes with butter, bacon, and maple syrup

"And I'll have two waffles, bacon, and two scrambled eggs."

"Thank you, gentlemen," the waiter said. "Your order should be right up."

"You believe everything Greg told us?" Tony asked Van after the waiter had left the table.

"I don't know," Van answered. "It doesn't fit the crime. Gettin' slapped don't equate to murder, if you ask me."

"Yeah, me either," Tony agreed. "And I don't like the fact that Greg never seen the homicide and doesn't know anyone who did see it. And then he won't even say who he heard it from?"

"Yeah," Van said. He took a sip of coffee and looked out the window. Then he smirked and added, "But at least we know he drives a white Honda."

The two detectives laughed as the waiter returned with their food. "Enjoy," he said as he placed their plates on the table.

"You think he's making it all up?" Van asked.

After he finished chewing, Tony said, "I don't know. But it definitely sounds a little flaky if you ask me. I mean, we'll still check out this Shorty guy. But for the murder, I just don't know."

"Yeah, I'm with you on that," Van agreed. They cleaned their plates, grabbed another cup of coffee, and then headed back to the house.

Chapter 5

When they arrived at the office after lunch, Tony shared the information Greg had given them with Detective Sergeant Richards. While he spoke to the sergeant, Van ran checks on the nickname, *Shorty,* and did a Department of Motor Vehicles check on white Hondas from the area in question.

Tony approached Van's desk a short while later. "Spoke to the sergeant," Tony told him.

"She thinks this guy is a waste of time?" Van asked as he leaned back in his chair.

"No, not that," Tony said hesitantly. "She just said to be careful with him because he's not a witness. She agreed that it all sounded a little flaky, and suggested maybe he's trying to throw us off, or that maybe he has a vendetta against Shorty for some other reason."

"True," said Van. "Hey. While you were updating the sergeant, I ran a DMV check on white Hondas. Guess how many hits I got from the Tilden area?"

"How many?"

"Twelve."

"You got twelve hits?"

"That's what I said," Van affirmed. "Twelve. I also ran a check on the name, *Shorty*. Fifteen hits from the Tilden projects on that one."

Tony laughed. "Guess there's a whole lot of short people over there, huh?"

"Seems that way," Van said, laughing.

"Any of 'em match our guy? Any matching the name, *Dave Wes*?"

"Nope. None."

"Maybe he has no felony charges because he just sells marijuana," Tony suggested. "Let me run an NCIC check on him and it should show misdemeanor arrests as well."

"When you're done, let's ride over to Alicia Lashay's house and ask her if she'd be willing to ride in a surveillance van to look for the perp."

"Alright," Tony agreed. "Give me ten minutes and this report should be done."

Ten minutes later, Van called out, "I got something on Dave Wes. Numerous charges for marijuana. No selling, but a lot for possession."

"He do any time?"

"No time."

"Just print a couple photos and we'll show them to Alicia as well," Tony suggested.

When they were done, they decided to head over to Alicia's house. Within a minute of arriving at the building, they heard a woman screaming.

"Help! Help! Somebody help me!" shouted a woman running straight toward them. "He's gonna kill me!" She ran right into the arms of Van.

"What's going on?" Van asked the woman.

"My husband gone crazy," she answered, breathing heavily. "He slapped and punched me in my face. He said I was the devil, and he had to kill me."

"Where's he at right now?" Tony asked.

"He's inside," she replied, pointing toward the apartment.

"Which apartment?"

"Apartment one-A," she answered.

"Okay," Tony said. "You stay out here, and we'll investigate. Does he have any weapons?"

"No," she replied, and then corrected herself. "Wait – he has a baseball bat."

"Where was he when you left the apartment?"

"In our bedroom."

"What's his name?" Van asked.

"Jose," the woman replied. "Jose Diaz."

"What's your name?"

"Arlene. Arlene Blanks."

"Okay. You stay right here, Arlene," Tony told her. "We'll go inside and get Jose."

"Okay," she agreed.

Tony spoke into his radio, "Homicide to central. Kay."

"Homicide. Kay," was the response.

"Central, be advised we have a ten fifty-one pickup of a black female with facial injuries caused by her husband," Tony reported. "We are at two six three eight Tremont Avenue, apartment one-A. We request a bus and additional units to respond. No emergency. Kay."

"Ten four," the radio operator confirmed. "Bus and additional units on the way. Kay."

"Also," Tony added, "be advised: myself and my partner are entering apartment one-A. Kay."

"Ten four. Use precaution. Kay."

Both officers drew their weapons and entered the apartment. Van called out, "Hello. This is the NYC police department. Jose, we're here to help you."

There was no response. They carefully approached the bedroom of the apartment with Van leading the way. The breaking of items and a man cursing and yelling incoherently could be heard from inside the room. Van signaled to Tony that the door was open and that he would cross to the other side.

From the other side of the doorway, Van could see a man facing the window with his back to the door. Tony came up to the side of the room, and both detectives pointed their guns in the direction of the man. Very calmly, Van said, "Hello, Jose."

Jose quickly turned around, face full of rage, and yelled, "Who are you? You're the devils who have come to kill me."

Van replied, still calm, "We're the police, and we're here to help."

Jose picked up the bat beside him and shouted at the detectives, "Come on and get me, if you can." He raised the bat and waved it over his head.

Van looked to Tony and quickly whispered, "I'm gonna close the door and grab my mace." Tony squinted and nodded to show he understood.

"When he comes out, mace him, and I'll knock the bat out of his hands," Tony said as he snapped opened his asp, a foldable baton that detectives used to assist with weapons.

"Bet," agreed Van.

In an instant, Van put his gun inside his holster, grabbed the door handle, and pulled it closed. Jose, still yelling and breaking things on the other side of the door, shouted, "I'll kill you devils! You won't take me to hell!" They could hear him charging toward the door, then heard a loud bang as the door shook.

"He's breaking the door handle," said Van, still holding the door closed. "You ready?"

Tony nodded and just seconds later, the door handle snapped off. Jose came out in a rage, holding the bat above his head in both hands. Van immediately maced him in the face, causing Jose to drop his left hand to cover his eyes. He was still holding the bat with his right arm, until Tony came down on it with the metal asp. Jose dropped the bat then, and Tony and Van dropped their weapons and took him to the ground. After Van quickly rear-cuffed him, he and Tony each grabbed Jose by one arm and took him out into the living room.

Both detectives were coughing from the mace in the air, but since they had closed their eyes, their sight wasn't affected. A few moments later, they could hear the radios of the responding cops and the voice of the victim just outside the apartment. Officers Robinson and Williams burst into the apartment with an EMS agent close behind.

"You guys alright?" Williams asked as Robinson briskly looked around the apartment.

"Yeah," Van answered, slightly out of breath. "This one is under for assault two and attempted assault of a police officer with a weapon. Can you take the bat and this perp to the house?"

"You got it," Robinson agreed.

They grabbed a hold of Jose and called the EMS agents over. "Do you want to take a look at this guy?" Williams asked.

One of the EMS officers approached Jose. "Are you alright, sir?" he asked him. "You need to open your eyes. I know it hurts, but the only way to get rid of the mace is to let the air dry your eyes."

"I can't open my eyes!" Jose shouted.

"Sir, your eyes are gonna keep watering because the ducts are trying to flush out the irritants," the officer explained. "You need to try and keep your eyes open as best you can. Do you understand?"

Jose didn't respond, but it seemed he was calming down and that reality was settling back in for him. His wife, Arlene, had been treated by EMS for a small cut on her lip and swelling and bruising under her right eye. As Robinson and Williams left for the house with Jose and his bat in evidence, Tony and Van took a moment to breathe. They looked at each other and smiled.

"Another fine job done by the dynamic duo," said Van.

"Yeah," Tony agreed, "we should be called Batman and Robin. But who'd be Batman?"

"Me!" they said simultaneously, and fell out laughing. They sat in silence for a few moments.

"Alright, who's catching?" asked Van.

"I guess you are," Tony answered.

They walked out into the hallway and EMS was still doing paperwork with the victim. When she was done, she looked up at Tony and Van and started to cry. "Thank you, officers," she said. "Especially for not hurting him or shooting him. He really is a good guy, except for smoking that darn dust. When he smokes it he just goes crazy, but this is the first time that he bugged out like that. He's never hit me before."

"You know PCP affects different people in different ways," Tony began to explain. "Caucasians just seem to get mellow, but people of color always get violent. It depends on how much formaldehyde they use." Arlene looked puzzled.

"Formaldehyde?" Tony repeated.

"What's that?" Arlene asked.

"It's embalming fluid," Van answered, having had a lot of experience with the chemical in his work as a mortician. "They use it in the morgue to keep dead bodies from deteriorating."

"Shut the front door," Arlene replied in shock. "You gotta be kidding me. That's what he's been smoking?"

"That's what he and thousands of others are smoking," said Van. "And not only is it affecting his mind, but it's also affecting his body."

"I didn't know that."

"Well, if you don't know, now you know," Tony kidded. "Isn't that how that song goes?"

"Yeah," Arlene answered flatly, still in shock.

"Let's lock up your apartment," Tony said. "We need to get over to the house so we can process this arrest."

She locked up her apartment and they left for the house. When they arrived at the house, Tony and Van escorted Arlene into the interview room and asked her to stay there for a while. Soon after their return, Detective Sergeant Richards came over to see how they were doing.

"You guys okay?" she asked.

"Yeah, Sergeant," Tony answered. "We're fine. It was just unexpected."

"Talking about collars for dollars," she teased, "I would have authorized overtime if I knew you guys were looking."

"We're always looking for OT, Sergeant," Van kidded back. "Just not like this. Too much paperwork! We got firearms discharge for the mace, and activation cards for the asp baton. But lemme tell you, that asp works like a charm." Van raised his hand in the air and Tony high-fived him.

"You got that right," Tony agreed. "And that mace does come in handy!" They laughed and high-fived each other again.

"You guys are crazy," replied Detective Sergeant Richards, shaking her head. "Go do your work."

As they walked past the holding cell, Tony and Van saw Jose, fast asleep. His right wrist was bandaged where Tony's asp had hit him, and his eyes were swollen closed from the mace. They passed the cell and entered the interview room to speak with the victim.

"Can we get you something to drink or eat?" Van asked. Since he had been the arresting officer, he took the lead with the questions.

"No," Arlene replied. "I'm fine."

"I just need to get some pedigree information, then you can write a statement for me alright?"

"Pedigree?" she asked.

Van explained that he needed basic identifying information from her and she complied, giving him her full name, date of birth, and address. As he always did during an interview or interrogation, Tony sat in so he could corroborate her statements.

"How long have you lived at that address," Van asked after recording her answers, "and who lives there with you? "

"About fifteen years," she answered. "Jose and my mother Irene live there with me."

"Are you married to Jose Diaz?"

"Well," she started, "we never got a certificate or nothin'. But I call him my husband."

"So, common law," Van noted. "Do you guys have any children?"

"We did have a boy, but we miscarried."

"I'm sorry to hear that," Van replied, looking up at Arlene for a moment.

"No worries," she replied. "It's been five years ago."

"How long have you and Jose lived at twenty-six thirty-eight Tremont?"

"Mmm," she thought for a moment, "'bout six years."

"Okay, so tell me what happened today?"

"Well," she started, "this morning when me and my mom got up, Jose was still sleeping. My mom said she had to go into work today and would see me later. I told her I didn't have to work today so I was gonna stay home with Jose." She paused and looked at Tony. "He just lost his job. So, my mom left and a few hours later Jose got up with this nasty attitude. We got into an argument because he said he wasn't gonna look for a job that day 'cause he was tired. So, he left the house and came back wasted, three hours later. I said to him if he didn't stop wasting his life away, he was gonna lose me. He just said *so what, then leave.* 'Then he went into the bathroom and I smelled this strange odor. I banged on the door and he flew out in a rage, calling me a devil. That's when he started hittin' me, so I broke away from him and ran into the hallway. That's when I saw you two."

"Okay," Van said. "I need you to write all that down for me – can you write and read?"

"Of course I can write and read!" Arlene replied loudly. "What do you take me for?"

"Don't take that the wrong way," Van said. "It's nothin' personal. But in the Bronx, there's a lot of people who can't read and write – you'd be surprised. It's just a question we have to ask. I'm sorry if it offended you."

"It's alright," she said. "I know you're just trying to help."

"So just write down your statement and I'll come back inside to check on you, okay?"

"Okay," Arlene agreed, and took the pen and pad from Van and started to write.

"I'll go update the sergeant," Tony told Van as they left the interview room. "You start your paperwork. After I talk to the sergeant, I'll get your perp and prep him for the arrest."

"Great," Van said.

Tony briefly explained to Detective Sergeant Richards what had transpired so far. When he left her office, he placed his gun in lockup and headed over to get Jose for processing. "Yo!" he shouted, tapping on the door. "Jose! Wake up."

Jose sat up and opened his eyes. It took him a few moments to realize where he was. "Hey detective," he said. "I'm really sorry for cussing and all that fuss."

"Do you remember what happened?" Tony asked.

"Yes. I do."

"Good," Tony replied. "So, am I going to have any problems with you? Can I take you outta this cell to get processed, or do I need my mace or asp again?"

"Is that some kind of joke?" Jose asked.

"You see me laughing?" Tony asked, straight-faced. "Ya see, from this point on, you better take everything I say to you seriously, because this is no laughing matter. You are being charged with felony assault on your wife, attempted felony assault on two police officers, residue of PCP, otherwise known as angel dust, possession of a weapon, and resisting arrest. You still laughing?"

"No," Jose said, putting his head in his hands. He wiped his face and looked up at Tony. "I'm really sorry for all that. I just lost my job. I lost my head."

"That ain't all you gonna lose," Tony told him. "I think you may have lost your wife and your home." Jose started to cry.

"Crying's a good sign," Tony added sympathetically. "There may be hope for you yet."

"I know I don't deserve her. I treated her so bad."

"I don't know if you deserve her or not, but I do know if you don't get some help, your life is going to mud. Goin' to jail may help you turn it around, give you time to reflect. You've got some serious charges, but whether you get serious time all depends on you. If you cooperate and don't give us any more trouble, my partner and I can reduce the charges. If your wife agrees, she can do the same and you could end up just getting thirty days. When you go to jail, if you keep your nose clean, you may end up doing just twenty-one days."

"Thanks, detective," Jose said. "Once again, I'm sorry I caused you stress. Can I see my wife?"

"Right now, no," Tony answered. "We gotta process you for this arrest, first. But I'll see if she wants to talk to you after that. You ready?"

"Yeah," Jose said. "Can I get a tissue to wipe my nose?"

"That, I can do for you," Tony offered. A minute later, Tony returned with a tissue. He handed it to Jose through the hole in the glass of the holding cell door. "Alright, turn around and place your wrist through the hole."

Tony handcuffed Jose and escorted him out of the cell. As they walked past Van, who was typing, Jose apologized to him as well. "Detective, I'm sorry for all this," he said. "Please forgive me." He dropped his head and started to cry again.

"Hey, Jose," Van said. "I'm not mad at you. It's that PCP. You just keep your head down when you go to jail and you'll be alright."

"Thanks, man," Jose said, still crying.

After taking Jose for prints, Tony brought him back to the holding cell and returned to the interview room to talk to Arlene.

"Hi, Ms. Blanks," Tony started. "Jose's back to normal now that the PCP has worn off. He apologized to me and my partner, and he wants to apologize to you. But I told him that's only if you want to see him."

"Well, I don't!" she said emphatically. "What can he say to me? That he's sorry? He won't do it again? I ain't trying to hear that. No, tell him when he gets out of jail, he can look for a new place to live. Tell him I'm tired of all this stuff he done put me through. I'm not gonna be his punching bag anymore. I don't care if he goes away for life."

"I know you're upset," Tony replied. "But it was the PCP that made him do those things."

"Well, then he shouldn't have done the PCP," she said. "I don't want to talk to him."

"I understand," Tony assured her. "I'll let him know. You ready to leave and go over to the Bronx criminal court building?"

"Yes. I am definitely ready to go."

"Alright," Tony said. "I'll go get uniformed officers to escort you over there, and we'll meet up with you there." He left the interview room and returned to the holding cell.

"What'd she say?" Jose asked immediately.

"Well," Tony began, "right now she's pissed and doesn't want to see you. Said she doesn't care if you get life right now".

"I really messed up, didn't I?"

"I'd say yes to that statement," said Tony. "But time heals all wounds. Give her some time, and you never know."

"I guess," Jose said. "I know I screwed up and I gotta accept my punishment."

"We'll be leaving shortly," Tony told him, and left to find Van.

Van was just getting up from his desk as Tony walked over. "Everything is just about done, partner," Van said. "Could you just voucher that bat for me?"

"Will do," Tony agreed. He took the bat and marked it with the initials, VM. He placed a brown paper bag around the bat and typed up an evidence voucher. He took it back over to Van's desk to get his signature on it.

"That should do it," Van said, and he and Tony walked over to the cell to get Jose so they could head to the courthouse.

When they arrived at the court building, Tony escorted Jose to central booking while Van sat with Arlene until their case was called. After processing Jose, Tony went upstairs to find Van and Arlene already engaged in conversation with the writing Assistant District Attorney. He signaled Van to let him know he was there, and went back into the hallway to review his notes on the homicide from the day before. An hour later, Van and Arlene came out of the ADA's office, and they left to take her home.

As they walked her to her apartment, she started to cry. "Thank you, guys, so much for treating me with respect," she said. "You really saved my life and I can't thank you enough."

"Don't worry about it, Arlene," Van said. "We just did our job. If Jose doesn't cop to the crimes, I'll need to get in touch with you for the grand jury. I do think he'll make a deal, but should you need anything anyway, here's my card. You just give me a call if you need to, okay?"

"Okay, Detective Morris," she said. "Thanks again."

"You're welcome," he replied.

"You take care," Tony said as Arlene shut the door to her apartment, and he and Van headed for the elevator.

Chapter 6

"Let's go see if Alicia's home and ask her about this guy, Shorty," Tony suggested." "We can also ask her exactly where Carl sold drugs in Harlem, and see if she'll take a ride up there with us."

"Sounds good to me, partner," Van replied.

When they arrived at her apartment, they each stepped to one side of the door, a habit learned from the attempted assassination of an officer before their time who had been shot in the face while standing directly in front of a door. Tony reached to the center of the door and knocked three times.

"Who is it?" a voice boomed from the other side of the door.

"It's Detectives Richards and Morris with the New York City Homicide Division."

The door slowly opened. "How y'all doing, Detective Richards? Please come in," Alicia greeted them. She turned from the door and led them into a small apartment with minimal furnishings and a foul odor. The living room had a small, two-seater love seat and two metal folding chairs. It was clear that Alicia was not much of a housekeeper. "Please, take a seat."

After each of the detectives sat down in a folding chair, Tony initiated the conversation. "Alicia, would you be willing to look at photos of possible perps and take a ride with us to Harlem?" he asked. "We'd like you to show us the area where Carl sold drugs. We'd be in an unmarked surveillance van and no one would know you were there."

"I don't know," she said, nervously. "That's a little scary."

"We'd be right there with you," Tony assured her. "And the van has one-way mirrors, so no one can see inside."

"You sure no one would see me?"

"I promise."

"Alright," Alicia agreed tentatively. "I guess I'll go with you guys."

"Fantastic!" Tony exclaimed. "Hey, you ever heard of a guy named Shorty?"

"No," she answered abruptly. "I don't know any Shorty. Why?"

"Just asking," Tony replied.

"What about Dave Wes?" Van added. "You ever heard of him?"

"Nope," she said matter-of-factly. "Don't know any Dave."

"Okay," Van said.

"So," Tony said as he rose from his seat, "tomorrow we'll pick you up and check out where Carl used to sell."

"What time should I be ready?"

"What about ten?" Tony asked. "Is ten good?"

"Yeah," Alicia replied. "Ten's good."

"Alrighty, then," said Tony. "We'll see you tomorrow at ten."

Alicia walked them to the door and promised again to be ready at ten.

When they were in the elevator, Van asked, "What's up with your girl, Tony? You think she's scared or just don't want to help us?"

"I don't know, man," Tony replied. "She seems concerned, but then again, she seems a little flaky."

"Yeah, I know," Van agreed. "Her man just got terminated and she's not asking any questions and don't seem too eager to help."

"Maybe we should be investigating her, Van."

In the car on the way back to the house, they reviewed all the things they needed to do, and agreed they needed to make a to-do list.

"There's a pen in the glove compartment," Van said. He almost always drove with Tony as his passenger. "You ready?"

"Yeah," Tony answered. "Shoot."

"Okay, we need to get more info on Shorty, take the wife over to Harlem, get more info on Bulldog," Van said, and rattled off a few more related items. "Then we need to speak with North narcotic units about Bulldog and about a surveillance van. Anything else I missed?" He looked at Tony.

"Nah, boss," Tony answered as they pulled in to the parking lot. "I think that's a lot to do for now."

"Then that's a wrap, I guess. I'll see you in the morning?" Van said, waving as both men headed to their cars.

"You bet. G'night!" Tony replied. "Oh, by the way," he shouted in afterthought, "Maddie has been asking me when you and Edith are gonna go out with us for dinner."

"How 'bout we go over to that nice Italian restaurant in Central Park? We can park our rides by the Central Park precinct."

"That sounds good. What time you wanna do dinner?"

"How about six?" Van suggested.

"Six it is, then! I'll let Maddie know."

"I'll tell Edith. She's gonna be excited."

"Alright. See you tomorrow."

"Good enough. Get home safe, Tony".

"You as well, Van," Tony said, and they headed home for the evening.

Chapter 7

The next morning, Van was working quietly at his desk when Detective Sergeant Richards arrived. "What's up, Sergeant?" Van greeted her. "How's it going?"

"I don't believe it!" she replied emphatically. "You beat Tony here?"

"I told y'all, it's a new day," Van answered. "This is a new me. From now on, I'm on time, every day."

"Well, shut the front door," Detective Sergeant Richards teased. "I guess I do believe you, now."

At that moment, Tony walked in and upon seeing Van at his desk, said, "Now I know that hell has frozen over." Detective Sergeant Richards burst into laughter.

"I told you guys I'm serious," Van defended himself.

"Alright, let's get this party started," Tony said, shaking his head in disbelief. "Can we have breakfast first? I'll treat, to celebrate the new you."

"Why not," Van answered. "We don't have to meet Alicia until ten. I'll just call Narcotics to arrange for the van to meet with us at an off-project location. Give me about ten minutes."

Fifteen minutes later, Tony called out, "Van, you ready to go?"

"Yeah."

"Okay, see if the sergeant needs something or wants to take a ride with us."

A few minutes later, Van told Tony that Detective Sergeant Richards wanted them to bring her back a coffee and bagel with cream cheese, and the partners headed out. At breakfast, they discussed their plans for the day and returned to the office an hour later with a bagel and coffee for Detective Sergeant Richards. After debriefing for a few minutes, she wished them well and they drove over to Alicia's house.

When they arrived at her apartment building, Tony called her. She explained that she still needed to drop the baby off at the sitter, so they waited another twenty minutes for her to come downstairs.

"Good morning, guys," Alicia said as she got into the car. "Sorry I'm late. I had to drop off Tanya."

"Good morning," Tony said in return. "We're gonna drive over to Southern Boulevard and leave this vehicle by the precinct over there and switch to the surveillance van." Alicia's eyes shifted from side to side and she started biting her fingernails. "Listen, the van looks just like a regular van," Tony assured her. "The difference is that the side windows are one-way mirrors, so no one can see inside. No one will be able to see you, and the forty-first precinct is also really far from where you live. Do you know anyone from that area?"

"No," she answered. "I don't think so. I guess it should be fine."

"Good," Tony said. "Then we're all set." He called Detective Leo Far with the narcotics unit and asked him to meet them at the precinct.

Twenty minutes later, they were parked outside the 41st precinct waiting for the surveillance van to arrive. While they were waiting, Tony showed Alicia some pictures they had picked up from the nicknames sheets. He had three books with photos attached to lists of nicknames and their associated real names and pedigree information. She claimed to not recognize any of the photos, and they wrapped up just as the van pulled up.

Alicia narrowed her eyes at the vehicle. "You were right," she said. "It looks like a regular van."

"See," Van said. "We told you there was nothing to worry about."

Detective Leo got out of the van and greeted everyone. He shook hands with the detectives first and introduced himself to everyone.

"I'm Detective Far with Narcotics," he said, making eye contact with everyone.

Tony extended his hand and said, "Detective Tony Richards. This is my partner, Detective Van Morris, and this young lady is Ms. Alicia Lashay. She's gonna be helping us out today." After they all shook hands, Detective Far ushered Tony, Van, and Alicia into the back of the surveillance van.

"So, this is how the van works. It just looks like any old van, so you guys just sit in here, no worries," Detective Far said, leaning into the van, and spinning one of the seats in demonstration. "The seats all have swivel ability, and there's a periscope that's camouflaged by the tin roof on top to just look like a vent." He tapped on the ceiling of the van twice.

"These," he paused as he tapped on the windows, "are mirrored from the outside, but as you can see, there's no obstructions from inside so you can see clearly out of them. Here's the switch to turn on the video camera," he said, pointing to a toggle that looked sort of like a regular light switch, "and this switch will take still pictures. Any questions?"

When nobody had any questions, Tony said, "Alright, then. We're good, so let's ride."

"Where to first?" Detective Far asked.

"Corner of 149th and Eighth, near a barber shop. Narcotics north said that's an area big on coke," Tony suggested.

"Is that where Carl sold?" Van looked at Alicia.

"Yeah," she confirmed, still looking very unsure of the situation.

"Alright," said Detective Far, "what I'll do is drive around the area for a minute and park. Then I'll walk around the block, find a location to hide, and you call me when you want me to come back so we can leave. Sound good?"

"Sounds good," Tony agreed, and Detective Far slid the door shut, hopped into the driver's seat, and drove off towards Harlem.

Chapter 8

Detective Far was able to easily find parking near 149th and 8th Avenues. After removing the key from the ignition, he turned towards the inside of the van and pretended to look for something.

"Okay," he said to Tony, Van, and Alicia. "We've got a lot of activity across the street by the barber shop. I'm gonna leave, but the interior air conditioner is running in quiet mode. Good hunting."

"Be careful," Tony advised him as he got out of the van.

He began walking west of where the vehicle was parked, on a typical city block with a lot of people in the area selling drugs. Once he was gone, a few guys walked over to the van and put their hands up to the glass to try to see inside. Tony and Van motioned to Alicia to be still and not say anything. She nodded in understanding.

A few seconds later, they walked away from the van. Tony then whispered to Alicia, "Very good. You were fine."

Van wrote down the address of the building next to their parking spot, 3333 8th Avenue. It was a barber shop named Donny's Cuts. Tony asked Alicia if she recognized anyone in the area from the shooting, but she shook her head in a definite *no*. He specifically asked her if she saw the guy she had described as Bulldog, but she again shook her head.

Then she whispered, "I'm scared. Can we please get outta here?"

"Sure," Tony replied, and he called Detective Far to tell him it was time to go. Three minutes later, Leo opened the door of the van, started it up, and pulled away.

As they headed back to the 41st precinct, he asked, "Did everything go okay?"

"Yeah," Tony answered. "It was good."

"Good," Detective Far said, but they drove the rest of the way in silence.

When they exited the van back at the precinct, Van held his hand out toward Detective Far. "Thanks, brother. You were awesome."

"Don't mention it," replied Detective Far as he shook Van's hand.

"Thanks, man," Tony said, also shaking Leo's hand.

"Yeah, thank you," Alicia chimed in.

"No problem," said Detective Far. "All you gotta do is forget this van and we'll be good."

"What van?" she said, smirking.

"That's my girl," Detective Far said, placing his hand on Alicia's shoulder. "You take care."

As Detective Far drove off, Tony patted Alicia on the back. "You did well today," he told her.

"I was so afraid," she said, shaking her head. "I'm so sorry."

"Don't be sorry," Van told her. "Because of you, we know exactly where Carl sold, and we have a place to continue this investigation. So, don't feel bad, 'cause you did good."

"That's right," Tony added. "It took a lot of guts to sit inside that van and be still when those guys walked up to the window."

"I guess," Alicia said.

"Well," Tony started, "you got nothing to fear when you're with us. It's our job to protect you. You want us to take you home or you have some other place you wanna go?"

"No, home would be fine."

"Alrighty, then," Tony said. "Home sweet home it is."

They all hopped in the vehicle headed back to Alicia's apartment. Once they got there, Tony began to talk to her about next steps.

"Now, if and when we make an arrest of the person responsible for Carl's death," he said, pressing the up button for the elevator, "you'll have to view a lineup. You'll be looking through another one-way mirror like the windows of the van today. The people on the other side of the glass won't be able to see or hear you."

Alicia nodded quietly. She started shifting her weight nervously from one foot to the other, and reached out and pushed the elevator button again.

"They'll be holding a sheet across their chest with numbers on it," Tony continued. "You'll have to tell us which one looks like the person you saw shoot Carl in this lobby. You think you can do that?"

"They won't be able to see me?" she asked.

"No," Tony answered emphatically. "They cannot see you, just like today when those two guys looked at the van. They'll just see a mirror."

"Yes," she said, seemingly to convince herself as much as the detectives. "I could do that."

The elevator opened and they all stepped in. When it stopped on Alicia's floor, Van held it open for her. She said goodbye to both detectives and opened the door to her apartment. Van immediately turned and looked at Tony.

"What the heck was all that about?"

"What?" Tony asked in response.

"What?" Van parroted. "She was terrified inside a van with two detectives? Something's not right. Do you buy that?"

"I don't know man," Tony said, scratching his head. "Maybe she was just really scared. Maybe she don't want to help us. I don't know."

"You think maybe she's got something to do with the hit?"

"No," Tony said with certainty. "I think she's just afraid. I think she's weak. I mean, she did run off and leave her daughter in the lobby."

"Yeah, you're right," Van said. "Maybe she's just scared. But who would leave their daughter and run off like that?"

"That's what I'm saying, man. I just think she's weak."

The elevator slid open and they stepped out into the lobby. They drove back to the house in silence and went to their respective desks to fill out some more DD5's. Tony finished his paperwork first, but waited for Van to be done so they could walk out to their cars together.

"We still on for tomorrow?" Tony asked.

"As far as I know, partner."

"Alright, see you tomorrow at about six."

"Tomorrow," Van answered, and gave Tony a goodbye salute as they each got into their cars.

Chapter 9

At 5:30 p.m., Tony and his wife, Maddie, pulled up in front of the Central Park precinct. He parked, placed an NYPD placard inside the window, and walked around to the other side of the car to help Maddie get out. As they walked toward the Central Park Restaurant, Tony craned his neck, looking around in all directions.

"Who are you looking for?" Maddie asked him.

"Van," he answered. "I should've known he was gonna be late, 'cause he's always late."

"Give him time. We're early, baby," Maddie assured him. "Jeez, you can't stand to be late for nothing, can you?"

"Whatchyu' talkin' 'bout, Willis?" Tony said with his lips pursed, and then broke into a wide smile.

"Well, am I right or what?"

"Yeah, yeah," he conceded. "When you right, you right!"

"I know," she said with a coy smile, and she put her right hand on Tony's cheek. They held hands as they continued through the park. The sun was just starting to set when they reached the restaurant, and they sat on a small bench while they waited for Van and his wife to arrive.

Ten minutes later, Van's voice echoed from just up the block. "Hey, hey, hey. Break it up," he teased upon finding them holding hands and laughing like teenagers.

"My man," said Tony as he stood, shook Van's hand, and slapped him on the back. "And who is this lovely young lady that you've coerced into accompanying you tonight?" Tony reached for the hand of the woman standing with Van.

"This would be my lovely wife, Edith".

"Hi," she said, smiling. "And thank you for the compliment."

"And this vision of beauty that you're with must be?" Van asked.

"Magdalena," Tony's wife answered, smiling and curtsying. "But my friends call me Maddie."

"Hi Maddie, this is my wife, Edith," Van replied, and the women shook hands and took turns greeting each other by name.

After all of the introductions were made, Edith said, "I'm so glad to finally meet you, Tony. I hear your name every other day from this one."

Maddie stuck out her thumb and jerked it several times in Tony's direction. "And I hear *your* husband's name *every* day from this one."

"You too?" asked Edith with a huge grin, and they all broke into laughter.

"I guess that makes us all family, right?" Van kidded.

"Well, family, let's go inside and get some of this grub I've heard so much about," Tony said, and walked into the restaurant.

"Tony Richards, party of four at six o'clock?" the maître d' confirmed. "Follow me, please, and I'll take you to your seats."

Just a few minutes after they were seated, the waitress appeared at their table. "Good evening folks welcome to Central Park," she announced confidently. "I will be your waitress tonight, and my name is Inez. Have any of you been here before?"

"No," Van replied right away. "We're all virgins." The look Edith gave him from across the table made it clear that she did not always appreciate his sense of humor.

"Well," the waitress replied, taking the comment in stride, "here at Central Park, we take pride in welcoming our first-time visitors. And to celebrate it being your first time, we provide a free sample of our fine wines. With that said, may I start anyone off with a nice red or white wine?"

Van said, "I'd like a chardonnay, please. And babe?"

"I would like a chardonnay as well," Edith replied.

"Chardonnay also, please," said Maddie.

"I better not rock the boat," Tony teased.

"So, four chardonnays," the waitress confirmed with a smile and a slight nod of her head, as she handed a menu to each of them. "I shall return shortly with your wine," she said, and she turned on her heels and left the table.

Maddie immediately said, "we're going to have rules here tonight, okay? There will be no job talk agreed?"

"You know," Edith said in response, "I knew I was going to like you before I even met you! That's right, men. No job talk."

The wives laughed out loud and high-fived.

"Well," Van said, half-laughing as he placed his hand on his chest in mock astonishment. "I guess y'all done told us."

"I mean, for real," said Tony, also chuckling to himself.

"Okay," Van said. "No job talk. So, what about them Knicks?" At that, they all looked at each other and started laughing.

The waitress returned to the table, smiling, and said, "I haven't even served the drinks yet!" They all fell out laughing again.

After a long evening of great conversation and a lot of good-natured teasing, they each ordered a cup of coffee. "You guys look like you really had a good time tonight," the waitress said as she placed the bill on the table. "Thank you so much for coming. I hope you come back again soon!"

"No, thank you, Inez," Van said as he picked up the check. "You have been fantastic tonight."

"Thank you," she said, and walked away.

"This one's on me. Next one's on you, buddy," Van said, pointing at Tony. "So, where we eating tomorrow night?"

After they all stopped laughing, Maddie said, "You know, this has been such a great dinner. I haven't had this much fun in a while. We have to get together at least once a month to do this."

"That sounds like a plan," Edith agreed. "This was great. We'll pick a new restaurant every month."

"And we'll split the bill right down the middle – in fact, let's start tonight," said Maddie.

"Not tonight," Van insisted. "I said I was paying for the meal and I'm paying. But we can start sharing the bill next month."

"Well, you better at least let me leave the tip," Tony said. "That way Maddie won't be mad at me, right Maddie?" He winked at her.

"He knows," she answered, matter-of-factly. "'Cause mama don't play that." They all started laughing again, and after rising from the table, they left the restaurant holding hands with their spouses, each of them eager to continue this newly started tradition.

Chapter 10

The next morning, Tony and Van arrived at the office at the same time. When they walked in, Sergeant Richards was already working.

"What's up, guys?" she asked. "How was your dinner?"

"It went quite well, matter of fact," Tony replied. "Our wives got along very well."

"They sure did," Van confirmed.

"Great – I'm glad they got along. What's the plan for today?"

"We're going over to Narcotics north to speak with the narco captain."

"Who's running the north team there?" asked Sergeant Richards.

"Captain Kahyle Ram," Van answered. "You know him?"

"No".

"Well, we're going to talk to him and see if he knows anything about this guy, Bulldog," Tony explained. "We're also gonna stop at the barber shop and see if we can get any info from anyone over there."

"Sounds good. Keep me posted, fellas."

"You got it, boss," Tony answered, and grabbed the homicide folder. He told Van he would meet him by the car. Once outside the office, he called over to North Narcotics and advised the captain that he was on his way. Van came down the stairs as Tony hung up the phone. He looked up.

"Looks like rain," he said. "You got an umbrella?"

"Sure do," replied Tony. "You?"

"Yeah. You're holding it."

"This little thing," Tony said, brandishing the small umbrella. "Man, you know the both of us ain't even gonna fit under this."

"Then I guess you better find another one."

"Well, you better find another one, 'cause this one's taken," Van said as he swiped at Tony's umbrella. They both got into the vehicle laughing and headed towards North Narcotics.

The unit was housed on the fourth floor of the U.S. Armory Building. When they walked in, several cops were typing, some were on the phones, and some were sitting around talking.

"Hey man," Tony said to one of the men who was by himself, typing at his desk. "Where's the captain's office?"

The man looked up from his typewriter. "Around the corner in the back," he replied with a smirk. "It's the door that says *Captain.*"

"Thanks," Van snapped back. "You got a headache thinking of that one, didn't you?"

Tony grabbed Van's arm. As he pulled him away, he said, "Come on, man. Don't waste your time on children."

"Yeah, you're right. His head is still probably hurting after that one."

They both walked away and found the office that read *Captain.* They knocked and a voice called out, "It's open. Just push."

Tony and Van pushed on the door and stepped into the office. The man behind the desk stood up and said, "I'm Kahyle Ram. And you are?"

"I'm Detective Tony Richards and this is my partner, Detective Van Morris."

"How are you guys doing?" the man asked, and he gestured towards two chairs in his office. "Please come in and take a load off. Have a seat and tell me how I can help you."

"Thanks, Captain Ram," Tony started. "We're here to talk about a homicide that we're investigating from the Bronx."

"From the Bronx?" the captain replied. "What does a homicide from the Bronx got to do with Harlem?"

"We believe that a person originally from Harlem, but who lived in the Bronx, got killed because he was selling in Harlem," Van explained.

"Wow," Captain Ram said. "Is that a stretch or do you have facts?"

"Right now, it's a stretch," Tony answered. "But with some strong facts to suggest that it's true."

"Alright, give me the facts."

"A guy named Carl White, black male, used to sell tin foils of coke at 149th and Eighth. We're being told this area is run by a guy named Bulldog, and supposedly Bulldog is the one who ordered the hit on Carl. We know it's a stretch, but the victim's wife believes this to be true. So, we came up here to see if you guys have a nickname file or have ever heard of this guy, Bulldog."

"We do have a nickname file," Captain Ram replied. "And I definitely know who Bulldog is."

"Really?" Tony said.

"Yes, really," answered Captain Ram, somewhat disinterestedly. "We've been after Bulldog for years. He's just a young punk, but he controls the north side of Harlem's cocaine industry. I know who he is, but he doesn't get his hands dirty. He lives up at three twenty-one Saint Nicholas. Kid's a wiz."

"What's his real name?" Van asked. "Ricardo Green". He's got top lawyers on retention and doesn't commit any crimes himself these days. We know he's the boss, but none of his guys will rat on him. Word on the street is he's taken out several perps. Those street rats are probably better off gone anyway." He laughed as he said this and added, "Bulldog's probably done us some favors, right? Taking out some of these perps so we don't have to." He laughed again.

"With all due respect, sir," Tony said, "a crime's a crime. And we're trying to get to the bottom of why Mr. White was murdered."

"Eh," Captain Ram responded, as he reached to peer through the window blinds beside him. He looked back at Tony and Van. "We can't get anything on Bulldog. We tried to get inside his organization, but he don't do business with people he don't know, and nobody talks. And no witness, no crime, right, boys? He's a dead end as far as we're concerned. But if you can get something on him and I can help, just give me a call. I'll go pull his file for you. Be right back."

Captain Ram stepped out of the office and Van looked at Tony in disbelief. "Tony," he whispered. "Did you hear this fool call the victims *perps* and *street rats*? And laughing about Bulldog taking them out?"

"Yeah, I heard old boy," Tony said, shaking his head.

"This dude's gotta be a racist," Van added.

"Nah," Tony replied. "He's just rude. Callous. Can't help himself."

"Well," Van said. "When you get the file on Bulldog, let's bounce. I'm done listening to this idiot."

"We will," Tony agreed.

The captain returned with a large file in his hand, and sat back down at his desk.

"Let me see," Captain Ram said as he shuffled through the papers inside the file. "Ah. Here we go. Yup. Name's Ricardo Green. Date of birth four, twenty-three, seventy-five. Residence is three twenty-one Saint Nicholas Avenue. Private house. Drives a ninety-six gold Mercedes Benz." He shook his head and laughed to himself before looking up at Tony. "You ready for his license plates?"

"I'm ready, Captain," Tony replied.

"One coke," he said, laughing out loud. "That's right. *One coke.* Some nerve, huh? This guy's a joke. But he's the Teflon Don up here in Harlem."

"What do you mean?" Van asked.

"Supposedly, Bulldog is responsible for four bodies and we can't find a single one. They all just disappeared. I'm sure nobody misses 'em," he added snidely. "But we call him the Teflon Don because we can't get anything on him. All I can say is good luck and I hope you get solid evidence on him. Anything else?"

"No," Van answered abruptly. Captain Ram looked at him inquisitively, and Van cleared his throat. "That should be all we need. Thanks, Captain."

"Alright," he answered. "Good luck, guys."

They shook the captain's hand and left the office. Van started in immediately when they got back to the car.

"What a knucklehead!" he exclaimed. "No wonder they can't catch Bulldog. That guy's a buffoon! A real idiot!"

"I know, I know," Tony agreed. "Let's head over to the barber shop and talk to Donny the Barber."

They drove over to 149th and 8th and parked in front of the barber shop. As soon as they got out of the car, the whistles started, warning everyone in the area that there were cops around.

Donny's was an old-time barber shop, with rickety chairs held together by duct tape. There were three people in the shop. One barber was in the middle of a haircut, and another barber was sitting and reading the paper.

"Welcome, gentlemen," the standing barber said without looking up. The seated barber looked up from his newspaper for a moment and, unimpressed, returned to reading. "Have a seat and I'll be right with you, unless you here for something other than a haircut."

"We are," said Tony. The reading barber looked up again. "Is Donny, the owner, here?"

"You speaking to him," the same man calmly replied. His eyes remained focused on his client.

"How are you, sir? My name is Detective Tony Richards, and this is Detective Van Morris. We're with the Bronx homicide squad."

"Bronx Homicide? You do know you in Harlem, USA, right?" Donny asked, amused. He chuckled as he looked up at the two detectives for the first time. "This is not the Bronx."

"Yes, sir," Tony replied. "We know."

"Alright, then," Donny said, smirking and shaking his head as he returned his attention to the haircut he had been working on. "How can I help you gentlemen?"

"Is there someplace in private that we could talk?" The seated barber again looked up from his newspaper.

"This is a barber shop," Donny said, matter-of-factly. "So, whatever you have to say, you can say it here in the open. Or, you could just leave. I'm trying to be nice. So, what do you want?"

"Do any of you know of a person by the name of Carl White?" Tony asked the three men.

"Why?" Donny asked.

"He was shot dead a few days ago, and I'm looking for anyone who knew him."

"Why you come to my shop for this?" Donny asked sharply, and he put down the razor he was holding. There was an instant change is his relaxed demeanor, and he took one step toward the detectives. "This ain't no library. We don't sell information here. This a barber shop where people get their haircuts, not talk about no Bronx killings. So, if that's all you come to find out, I suggest you go someplace else."

"Sir," Van said, "you didn't say whether you knew him or not."

"That's right. I didn't say! But what I am gonna say is would you two please leave my barber shop now!"

"No problem, sir," Van answered.

"And if there's anything that you decide you would like to talk about, I'll just leave my card right here," Tony said, placing a business card on the small table next to the door. "If you call, your information will be kept between us.

"Thanks," said Donny, and with that, they left the barber shop.

"What was that all about?" Van asked as soon as they got back into the car.

"I know," Tony said. "He came off very strong. He didn't even let us get into why we were there."

"You think he's trying to tell us something?"

"I don't know but his behavior was kind of strange, wasn't it?"

"Maybe he'll give us a call."

"I don't know," Tony said. "But he was in a hurry to get us out of there. We'll just have to wait and see. Let's go over to Carl's mom's house. She's just a few blocks up at the next project."

They drove over to 3220 8th Avenue and parked the car. They took the elevator up to the fourth floor and knocked on the door of apartment 4A.

"Who is it?" asked a high-pitched voice from the other side of the door.

"Detective Richards, Homicide Squad."

The door opened just a bit and a teenage girl peered out. "Hi," she said shyly.

"I'm Detective Robinson and this is my partner Detective Morris."

"How you doin'?" Van greeted the girl.

"I'm fine," she said. "You can come in and speak with my mom."

"And who might you be," Tony said, "if you don't mind me asking?"

"I'm Aleya. Carl's younger sister." She turned from the detectives and led them into the living room.

It was furnished with old, mismatched pieces, but the house was very clean. Another young girl, a bit older than Aleya, was sitting on the couch with her legs folded and feet under her. An older woman was sitting in a wide chair with a glass of iced tea on a small table next to her. A game show was on the television.

"Good afternoon, ladies," Tony started, and then focused his gaze on the older woman. "Are you Ms. Ann White, mother of Carl White?"

"Yes, I am," she confirmed. "Who wants to know?"

"I'm Detective Richards and this is my partner, Detective Morris. We're with the homicide squad and we would first like to offer our condolences."

"Wait a minute," Ann snapped. "You're the ones investigating my son's death? And you're just getting here today?"

"Yes, ma'am," Tony confirmed. "And I'm sorry. But we have been quite busy with this investigation. I assure you, we have been working on it and I do apologize for not coming or calling sooner."

"You doggone right," she retorted, suddenly angry. "You shoulda *been* done called me! I'm his mother! He was my son. And *now* you come over here. What do you want?"

"I certainly understand your frustration, Ms. White," Tony said. "But like I said, we have been working non-stop on this investigation. We're moving right along and, with your help or your kids help, we may be able to close this case with an arrest."

"Ma, you need to stop talking like that," said the older girl. "These detectives did come over to see you. They didn't kill Carl, and they're here to help."

"Thank you," Tony started, "Miss...?"

"Yazmin," she said. "I'm Carl's other sister." She was about seventeen, but sounded much more adult than her mother.

"Thank you," Tony replied. "May we sit?"

"Yeah, have a seat," Ann said. "I'm sorry, Detective Richards. This was just all unexpected. I told that hard-headed boy not to get into the drug game. Told him someone was gonna kill him. He didn't believe me. I bet he believes me now, don't he?

"Who gonna raise his Tanya now? Lord knows I can't. What am I supposed to do?" she called out as she started to cry and yell. "Lord, help me! Help me, Lord! I need you, Lord."

Aleya walked over and cradled her mother's head. "Don't cry mom," she said as she stroked her hair. "Don't cry. It's gonna be alright."

"Ms. White," Van said. "Sometimes life is hard. When you lose a loved one, you feel the world's going to end. But the bible says,*great in the sight of the Lord is the death of his saints* And, in God's eyes, Carl was still one of his saints." Van flashed a sideways glance at Tony, who was trying his best not to roll his eyes.

Still wiping her eyes, Ann loudly cried, "you're right, Detective. He was trying to feed his family. I just wish he had found another way to do it."

"I wish the same, Ms. White," Van continued, and he reached out to lightly touch Ann's back in a show of support. Tony subtly shook his head. "But even if he may have done wrong in the sight of the law, he was still a child of God.

And we will do the best that we can to put away the murderer, if you ladies can help us out."

"Oh, thank you, Detective Morris," Ann sobbed. "You're right. What can we help you with?"

Tony stepped in and said, "The first thing that we need is some background on this area. We're Bronx detectives, and we don't usually work here in Harlem."

"What kind of information do you need?" Ann asked.

"Who runs the coke in this area?" Tony asked. "And who would want to stop Carl from selling here?"

"Bulldog," said Yazmin without hesitation. "I heard he had beef with Carl about selling in his neighborhood. He runs coke from 139th up to 149th. And he told Carl to stop selling or he'd put a stop to it for him. Carl told him this was a free country and that no one owned slaves anymore and that there was enough business out here for both of them. Bulldog told him he wouldn't get a second warning, so Carl bought himself a gun and started carrying everywhere."

"Do you know who this guy Bulldog is?" Van asked. "Do you know his real name?"

"No, I only know him as Bulldog. And I told Carl to just go someplace else and sell. I told him to look for another job, too, and leave that coke stuff alone. But he said he wouldn't stop until he made enough to get mom and us and him and Alicia and the baby out of these projects. He thought that was his way out. Then we hear he got shot in the head."

"You know what Bulldog looks like?" Tony asked.

"Yeah. He always drives a gold Mercedes. I heard he even has a gold gun."

"A gold gun?" Tony asked.

"That's right," Yazmin confirmed. "Real gold. At least that's what they say."

"You ever seen the gold gun?"

"No, but I wouldn't be surprised if he really does."

"What does he look like?" Tony asked.

"He's in his twenties," Yazmin answered. "About six-foot, light-skinned. Black Hispanic. He looks good. He's got a crew cut."

Tony's cell phone buzzed in his pocket. He took it out to look at the number, and placed it back into his pocket. "Does he have a crew?"

"I don't know who, but there's always drug dealers going over to his car and dropping off cash."

"What's happening over by the barber shop," Van asked.

"Donny's? That's where Carl set up at," she said. "He would wait right out front and pitch his coke. Whenever the cops came he'd just walk over to the barber shop and pretend to be waiting to get a haircut."

"Did he ever get arrested?" asked Tony.

"Nope. He only sold to people he knew, and he cut two dollars off what everyone else charged. That's why he did so good."

"Where did he get his coke from?"

"Uptown in Washington Heights. He never told us who or the exact place he'd go to get it. I do know it was from some guy he used to serve when he worked at the meat market."

"This is good," Tony said. "All this information is gonna help with our investigation."

"Do you think you'll make an arrest for my brother's murder?"

"So far, I haven't had any homicides left open," Tony assured her. "I'm not promising you that I can make an arrest on your brother's case, but I will definitely do my best. Do you ladies have any more questions for me or my partner?"

"No questions, officers," said Ann, who had been quiet the entire time that Yazmin spoke to the detectives. "No, but I just want to apologize for snapping at you earlier. I wasn't in my right mind."

"That's okay, Ms. White," Tony said. "We get much worse. Don't worry about it."

"Thank you," she repeated. "So much. I do hope you make an arrest."

"We do too," said Van. "And once again, we are very sorry for your loss."

The detectives rose from their seats and thanked each of them, and walked towards the door. Yazmin walked them out of the apartment and into the hallway, and asked that they contact her if they discovered anything.

As they entered the elevator, Tony looked at Van and said, "Guess who called me when we were in there?"

"Don't tell me," Van replied. "Donny, the barber."

"Bingo," said Tony.

"What do you think he wants?"

"I don't know, but I'm gonna find out when we get downstairs."

As promised, Tony took out his phone as soon as they stepped out of the elevator. He pressed redial for Donny. The phone rang and Donny answered. Tony put his phone on speaker so Van could hear.

"Hello? Who this?"

"This is Detective Richards calling. I'm returning your phone call. How can I help you?"

"Oh, hey. It's how can I help you," Donny said. "Sorry for the way I treated you guys when you showed up at my shop today, but I had to act like that. A couple of Bulldog's guys was watching you, so I didn't want to say too much. When you left, they came over and asked me why you were there."

"Who are these guys you're talking about?" Tony asked. "You know their names?"

"I'd feel better if I could come to your office and talk. Is that possible?" Tony looked at Van and Van nodded in approval.

"Sure," Tony said. "What time can we pick you up?"

"I'll come by," Donny replied. "The address on the card, right?"

"Yeah, that's the one. What time should we be expecting you?"

"How 'bout ten? That okay?"

"Yes, ten is fine."

"Alright, then," Donny said. "I'll see you guys tomorrow."

"Okay, see you at ten tomorrow," Tony confirmed and hung up the phone.

"He was frontin' the whole time we were there," Van said.

"Sounds like it," Tony agreed. "We'll see how he is tomorrow. Let's get out of here."

They drove back to the homicide squad and went upstairs. Detective Sergeant Richards greeted them when they arrived. "Hey guys," she said warmly. "How did it go?"

"Well," Van started, shooting a disgusted glance towards Tony. "We met the captain of Narcotics and I'm still trying to figure out how he ever made it to captain."

"Why? What happened?" she asked, and looked at Tony.

"He just had an air about him," Tony explained. "Said Bulldog killed a number of *perps* for us. Then he said Bulldog did us some favors by killing *street rats,* and said no one would miss 'em... I don't think he ever used the word *people* or *person,* and he laughed at it all."

"He sounds like an idiot," Detective Sergeant Richards said.

"That's exactly what I said," Van replied.

"Yeah, you did say what an idiot he was," Tony agreed, half laughing. "He did give us some pertinent information, though. He gave us pedigree info on Bulldog. His real name's Ricardo Green, he's a black Hispanic, runs the north side of Harlem's coke business. Twenty-two years old, drives a gold Benz, and they can't get a buy on him because he doesn't handle product and won't sell to people he doesn't know. Told us he lives in a brownstone on Saint Nicholas Avenue in the Sugar Hill area and that it's rumored he's committed several homicides, but they can't find the bodies."

"That is good information to start with," Detective Sergeant Richards agreed. "Where'd you go from there?"

"After leaving North Narcotics, we drove over to 149th and Eighth to a barber shop owned by a guy named Donny. He didn't give us his last name and at first, he was very rude. Later on, though, he called me and apologized, and said Bulldog's boys were watching us in the shop. He's coming to the office to tell us what he knows tomorrow."

"Busy day," Detective Sergeant Richards commented.

"We haven't even gotten to the best part yet," Van added. "After we left the barber shop, we went over to speak with the mother of the deceased. We met his two younger sisters."

"Sergeant," Van said and started laughing. "You shoulda heard this woman. She was like a bat outta hell. She was doggin' us like nobody's business at first. Then, you know your boy. I had to pull the God card on her."

Detective Sergeant Richards dropped her head and covered her face.

"Yes, Lord!" Van shouted. "Yesss, the Lord is looking over you." They all fell out laughing at his exaggerated gestures.

"You need to stop, Van," Detective Sergeant Richards warned lightheartedly.

"So," Tony began as he stopped laughing and looked at Van accusingly. "As I was saying, before I was *rudely* interrupted, we went to Carl's mother's house. Her daughter, Yazmin, was very forthcoming with information about her brother and Bulldog. She thinks Bulldog killed him because they had beef about selling in his area. She doesn't know for sure, but she definitely believes he did.

"Man, you guys really were busy today, huh?"

"If you don't work, you don't eat," Van stated, and then added, "as per the Bible."

"Here we go, Mr. Bible scholar," Tony said as he rolled his eyes.

"Hey, you reap what you sow," Van replied.

"Man, would you quit it?"

"Alright, alright," said Sergeant Richards. "Great job guys, for real. We'll pick this up tomorrow. You two have a good night."

Chapter 11

The next morning, Detective Sergeant Richards came into the office to check up on the progress Tony and Van had made.

"Good morning, guys," she greeted them. "How's it going?"

"We're fine, Sergeant," Tony responded. "Just getting information on Bulldog. I'll inform you when you settle in."

"Great," she answered, and headed to her office.

"I ran a background check on Donny's barber shop," Van said. "Got nothing. Also ran a check on Carl's siblings. Also nothing."

"Alrighty, then," Tony replied. "Sounds like breakfast time to me."

After a one-hour breakfast break, Tony and Van returned to the office, eager to meet with Donny. At ten o'clock, Tony got a call from the desk officer to let him know he had a visitor downstairs. Tony told the desk officer to send him up, and a few minutes later, Donny walked in wearing blue jeans, a blue t-shirt, white Puma sneakers, and a blue Yankees cap.

"Good morning," Donny said, wiping his hands on the sides of his jeans.

"Hey, Donny," Tony answered. "How ya doing?"

"What's up, sir?" added Van.

"Nuttin'," Donny replied, still anxiously playing with his hands.

"Come on in here," Tony said, motioning to the interview room. "We can sit and talk in here. You need anything to drink?"

"No, I'm good," Donny said, and he followed Tony into the room.

Van entered last and closed the door behind them as he pulled up a chair directly next to the only table in the room. Tony sat down directly across from Donny. "First I'm going to need your pedigree. What's your full name?" Tony asked, taking the lead on the interview.

"Donald Henry," he replied. "Friends call me Donny."

"Your age?"

"I'm sixty-one."

"Address?"

"Thirty-three thirty-three Eighth Avenue. Apartment fifteen C."

"How long have you been living there?"

"Fifty-nine years," Donny said emphatically.

"Wow," Van commented. "That's longer than I've been alive."

"I love Harlem," Donny said. "I've seen it go through lots of changes, and I've come through without any scratches, thank God."

"He's the one to thank," Van added with a smirk and a quick glance at Tony. Tony flashed a look back that clearly said *don't start that again*

"Okay," Tony continued. "Should I call you Mr. Henry or would you prefer Donny?"

"Donny's fine."

"Okay, Donny, tell us what you know."

"Well, I don't know who killed him, but I did know Carl. He grew up around the way and would come to my shop for his haircuts like most of the neighborhood kids. He was a good guy. He got into a little trouble here and there, but nothing major. Had a baby a little over a year ago. He was feeling the pressure, so he started selling drugs in the neighborhood. Now I told him Bulldog was gonna get mad if he kept selling out there in front of the barber shop. But he ain't listen to me, as you can clearly see."

"Do you know Bulldog's real name?" Tony interjected.

"Sure, I do. Don't y'all?"

"We work in the Bronx, so we don't know much about Harlem and the drug game over there."

"Well, everybody in Harlem knows Bulldog. Ricardo Green. He lives up in Sugar Hill. Drives a gold Benz. Young cat, just about twenty-two. I do believe Bulldog had something to do with Carl's death. Now I ain't saying he did it, but bet your bottom dollar, he at least knows who did."

"How do you know he killed Carl?" Tony asked.

"Like I said," Donny reiterated, "I *don't* know for sure. But word on the street is Bulldog *had* him killed 'cause he dissed him. I also heard Bulldog's got a couple more bodies to his rep."

"Do you know his crew?" Tony asked.

"Who you mean? Seven, Kool, and Light?" Donny half-laughed as he shook his head. "Them boys is crazy, man. I believe all them dudes done killed before. They all grew up in the neighborhood. All about the same age. Seven's name is Jason, Kool's name is Zak, and Light's name is Jules. They all been arrested and did time. Out of all them guys, though, Light's the craziest. He'll shoot you if you look at him wrong." "What are their last names if you know?" "Jason Rite, Zak Black, Jules Brown."

"Did Carl ever have words with any of them over selling in that area?"

"Maybe," Donny said, shrugging his shoulders. "You know what? Light usually worked in the area where Carl was selling at. But I haven't heard anything like that. Maybe Light shot Carl. Maybe he didn't. I don't know."

"Well, Donny," Tony said as he pushed back from the table in his chair. "All the information you've given us is a trove of knowledge. People like you make our job easier, so thank you for coming in and sharing with us."

"Thank you," Donny returned. "And again, I'm sorry we started off the way we did."

"Don't worry about it," Tony replied. "Do you need a ride back up to Harlem?"

"No, I drove over here. But thank you."

"Alright, well, if you need anything from me, don't hesitate to call."

"Thanks, Donny, for all your help," said Van.

"No problem. Glad I could help. Good luck with your investigation."

"Thanks, Donny," Tony said as Donny walked out of the office. He looked at Van. "You ready to decipher all this information?"

"Yeah," Van replied. "This is the second time someone said Bulldog has some bodies to his name. We need to check on that."

"Bulldog's definitely looking like a good candidate," Tony said. "We got last names on his boys now. But that nickname,*Light* You remember Carl's wife, Alicia, said the man who shot Carl had real light eyes."

"She did," Van confirmed. "And let's call the local precinct and find out if they have any reports of missing persons with drug ties. We'll also need to check on getting TIPS posters printed up on Carl so we can post them at Tilden projects and the surrounding area."

"We also need to do a BCI check on the nicknames," Tony added. "I'll be ready to go in five, if you're ready."

"Ready when you are," Van replied.

At headquarters, they each went to separate departments. After Van got the nickname checks on the BCI computer, he went upstairs to the TIPS office where Tony was waiting to check on getting posters made.

"You still waiting?" Van asked.

"Yeah, but they should be done in about fifteen minutes. What'd you get from BCI?"

"I got real names and arrest records on all of 'em," Van answered. "Seven, real name is Jason Rite. Black male, twenty-one years old, eight narcotics arrests, and two robbery assaults. Kool's real name is Zak Black. Black male, twenty-one, all the same arrests as Seven, acting in concert. And last, but not least, Light. Real name is Jules Brown. Black male, twenty-two years old. Again, same arrests as the other two guys, also acting in concert. Now," Van paused dramatically, and looked at Tony for effect.

"Alright, alright," Tony said, playing along. "What is it?"

"It is," Van started, "the pièce de résistance Bulldog. Real name, Ricardo Green. Black male, twenty-two, and wouldn't you know, the exact same arrests as the other three. All acting in concert."

"So, let me guess," Tony said. "They all came from the same neighborhood and lived near each other, right?"

"Close," Van said. "They didn't just come from the same neighborhood. They lived in the same building."

"Shut the front door," Tony kidded. "You've gotta be kidding me."

"Nope. Three two two five Eighth Avenue. Seven lived in two A, Kool lived in four C, Light lived in seven D, and Bulldog lived in apartment eleven A. How you like me now?"

"Man, I would have never guessed that these boys grew up robbing and dealing. No wonder they're so tight and don't rat on each other. They family."

The TIPS officer stepped out into the hallway. "Detective Richards," he yelled.

"We gotta go over to the housing authority and find out if their relatives are still staying in those apartments," he told Van, and then raised his hand at the TIPS officer as he stood to greet him. "Right here."

"Here are your posters," the TIPS officer said as he handed the stack of eleven- by twenty-inch papers to Tony. "Look them over and see if they have all the information you requested."

At the top of the posters it read,*REWARD: Up to $1,000 in cash for information leading to the* *arrest and or indictment of the person(s) responsible for the death of Carl White.*Below the text was a picture of Carl, smiling and wearing a white t-shirt. The details and location of his death were also listed on the posters, as well as the number to call to share information.

"This looks great," Tony said to the TIPS officer.

"Thanks," he replied, and gave a small salute to Tony and Van.

"Take care, Detective. Good hunting," "Thanks," Tony said to him, and he and Van went downstairs and out to the car.

"Where to?" Van asked.

"Let's take a ride up to Harlem and speak with the Housing Authority manager," Tony suggested, and they headed over to the projects manager's office and went inside.

"Hello," Tony greeted the woman at the reception desk. "I'm Detective Richards and this is Detective Morris. We're here to speak with the manager."

"Ms. Akeena Rell?" she asked politely.

"Yes."

The receptionist picked up the receiver of her desk phone and pressed a large button on the keypad. "Ms. Rell," she started, pausing briefly for the response on the other end. "There are two detectives here to speak with you."

The receptionist hung up the phone and flashed another smile at the detectives. "Just walk down the hall. It's the third door on the right."

"Thank you, ma'am," Tony said, and he and Van headed down the hall. They knocked on the closed door.

"Come in," called a woman's voice from the other side of the door.

"Hi," Tony said, as he and Van entered the office. "I'm Detective Tony Richards and this is my partner, Detective Van Morris."

"How are you guys doing?" the woman asked. "I'm Akeena Rell, the Saint Andrews Housing Authority manager. How can I help you?"

"We're from the homicide squad in the Bronx and our investigation has brought us to your project. We're hoping you can help us by providing some family history on several of your members."

"I'd be glad to help. What do you need?"

"The first family we'd like information on is the Green family."

"Sure," Ms. Rell said, and she began alternately typing and looking through file folders on her desk. "Let me see. Green. Okay. Here you go. Mother is Elaine Green. Black Hispanic female, fifty-seven years old. She had one son named Ricardo Green. Still lives at thirty-two twenty-five Eighth Avenue, apartment eleven A. Just her in that apartment. Next?"

"Rite is the last name," Tony told her.

"Rite," she repeated back to him, and began searching in the same manner as she had for the Green family. "Here. Got it. Alyssa Rite, black female. Fifty-four, one son, two daughters. Still lives at thirty-two twenty-five Eighth Avenue, apartment two A."

"And just the son's name?" asked Van.

"Jason Rite."

"And then we've got Black and Brown," Tony said.

"Black, right here. Sharisse Black," Ms. Rell clarified. "Black female, fifty-five, three daughters, and one son, Zak Black. Still lives there, same building, apartment four C.

"And, next, Nina Brown. Black female, fifty-five, one son, Jules Brown. She," Ms. Rell furrowed her brow and paused for a moment. She looked at another piece of paper. "Ms. Brown no longer lives in the building. She's now at two six four two Tremont Avenue, apartment seven E in the Bronx. She's in your neighborhood now," she concluded with a smile.

"Thanks a lot, Ms. Rell," Tony said.

"You're very welcome. Anything else I can help with?"

"No, that's all."

"Well, thank you for coming by, and good luck with your investigation. If there's anything else that you need, don't hesitate to call."

"Will do," Tony assured her. "Goodbye now."

"Take care, gentlemen."

They left the office and got in the car. Van said, "You think those guys still live over here?"

"Yeah," Tony answered. "Why leave if you run the joint? Why spend the money? Bulldog only moved to Sugar Hill to flaunt his wealth, and it seems he's got way more than these guys. I mean, a gold Benz and a gold gun? Who does that?"

"Scarface," Van replied, laughing. "Seems that's who Bulldog thinks he is."

"Yeah, well," Tony said, shaking his head. "He's about to be taken off his throne just like Scarface."

"Say hello to my little friend," Van replied.

Tony laughed and said, "Let's get out of this crazy town and back to the house."

When they got back to the house, they went straight upstairs. Van started on his DD5s immediately while Tony visited the sergeant to update her on what they had so far. After updating her, Tony went to his desk and started his DD5s. When their paperwork was done, they called it a night and each headed home.

Chapter 12

Van was already working when Tony got to the office the next morning.

"I just got a call from the ADA's office," Van told him as soon as he walked in. "Jose Diaz. He isn't fighting the charges. He's copping to two years."

"Wow," Tony said. "Well, at least Arlene doesn't have to worry about going to the grand jury."

"Yeah, or worry about him hurting her."

"I don't know about that," Tony said. "He'll probably do a third, get out, and go right back to Arlene."

"I don't know," Van replied. "She sounds like she's done."

"Maybe," Tony said. "Anyway, what you got?"

"Let's go over to Tilden and put up the posters, then go talk to Alicia again about Bulldog."

"Okay, but our first stop is breakfast, right?"

"Right," Van agreed, and they headed out.

Their first stop was the 161st Street Diner for breakfast, and then they drove over to the Tilden projects. They got out of the vehicle and walked over to 2638 Tremont Avenue to hang the posters. "Let's put them over by the elevator," Tony suggested as he scanned the lobby. "Everyone who walks in the building will see it."

Just as they started to hang their first sign, the rear door of the building slammed closed. They turned towards the sound as a man walked into the lobby. He was a young, black guy with a blue t-shirt, blue jeans, and white sneakers. He looked around anxiously and asked, "You two the detectives assigned to this homicide?"

"Yeah, why?" Tony replied.

"I've been trying to get to talk with you guys. I know the guy who killed Carl," the man said. "But I can't talk here. Too many people know me and I don't want it to get around that I ratted."

"You want us to meet you someplace else so we can talk?" Van asked.

"Yeah, but not around here. Can you meet me up the hill on Castle Road in twenty minutes?"

"We can do that," said Van.

"Alright, cool," the man said, and he left in a hurry.

"What do you make of that?" Van asked Tony as they continued to hang the posters.

"I really don't know, man," Tony said. "This could be another mislead. Like that guy, Greg, the other day. That went nowhere."

"Yeah, that's what I was thinking," Van agreed.

"We probably should have asked his name," Tony added, laughing. "But we won't know for sure what it's worth unless we take a chance."

"Alright, let's do this."

They drove over to Castle Road and parked the car. Moments later, they recognized a man walking towards the back of their car as the same man from the lobby. They both exited the vehicle.

"Hey, man. Stop right there," Van said calmly, and the man immediately stood still. "Sorry to have to do this, but we don't know you, and you don't know us. So, to be on the safe side, we're gonna need to frisk you before you can get in the vehicle. Is that gonna be alright?"

"Sure," the man said. "I don't carry weapons and I don't have any drugs on me."

"Okay, step forward and put your hands on the vehicle," Van instructed. "Place your legs back towards us, and spread your legs." Van approached him and patted him down, first on his left side and then his right. Tony kept his eyes on the man to make sure he didn't make any sudden moves, and when Van was done, Tony told him to get in the back of the car.

Tony and Van got into the car and turned around to face the man. "I'm Detective Tony Richards and this is my partner, Detective Van Morris. What's your name?"

"Brandon Night," the man said. "I knew Carl and I also know the person who shot him."

"Whoa," Van said. "If you have information about this homicide, why are you just telling us now?"

"I was there the day Carl died," he started. "I tried to tell a cop outside the building that I saw who shot Carl. But he just told me to move along, so I said the heck with you too, and I left."

"An officer at the scene of the crime told you to move on?" Tony asked.

"That's right."

"That was probably before we told them to get names of everyone standing outside," Van suggested.

"Yeah, I'd like to believe that," Tony said. "But who knows? Anyway, I'm sorry, man. Here's what we're going to do. We're gonna drive you over to the homicide squad for an interview now if you have time."

"I do," said Brandon.

"Great," Tony said. "And we'll give you a ride back over here when we're done." Brandon agreed and they drove over to the homicide squad to start the interview.

Chapter 13

Upstairs in the interview room, Tony asked Brandon to have a seat while he and Van visited Detective Sergeant Richards. They let her know they had returned with a witness and quickly returned to the interview room.

"Before we get started," Tony began, "I need to get your pedigree. What's your full name, age, and place of residence?"

"Brandon Night," he answered. "I'm twenty-seven. I live in Tilden projects at two four oh five Pebble Street, apartment six G."

"How long have you known Carl White?"

"About three years. I just knew him from the area. We'd say hi when we saw each other."

"Tell me what you know about the homicide."

"The day of the homicide, I was coming into the building to visit with a friend who lives on the third floor," said Brandon. "I usually come in the back because my building is on the opposite side. And while I was walking up, I heard several loud bangs."

"How many?"

"About four, I think. Then the back door opens and there's Light, holding a gun and putting it in his pants under his hoodie. He looked up and said *what's up, Brand,* and then he skipped off towards his building. When I got to the lobby, I saw Carl on the floor with a pool of blood around him. Then the police ran inside as I got to the front. Then they wouldn't let anyone else in the building. I walked up to this cop and I tried to tell him I saw the killer, but he told me to move on, so I did."

"Okay," Tony said. "I have a couple questions for you."

"Go ahead."

"Alright, first, who's Light?" Tony asked.

"Light's his street name," Brandon answered. "We call him that 'cause of his eyes. They're real light. I've known him about four years. His real name is Jules Brown, but he don't like to be called Jules. Says it sounds too white."

"Do you know where Light lives?"

"Yeah. He lives in Tilden projects at twenty-six forty-two Tremont."

"What was Light wearing that day?"

"Black hoodie and blue jeans. White sneakers. He also had his three eighty nickel with him."

"You saw the gun?"

"Yeah," Brandon confirmed. "In fact, two days before, I saw him by the side of the building with two other guys I didn't know. He had the gun then, too. I walked up to him because we was playing basketball the day before, and we got into an argument. I went over to him to make sure we were cool. I saw the gun inside his waistband, but he said, *don't worry, it ain't for you.* I told him I just wanted to make sure we were alright. He gave me a high five and said we were cool, so I left."

"Could you identify the other two males if we showed you photos?" Tony asked.

"Yeah, I think so."

"That poster I was putting up in the lobby is a TIPS poster," Tony added. "If you give your testimony, you can claim the thousand dollars they're offering."

"For real?"

Tony nodded and said, "If you're willing to testify against Light."

"I'm willing," Brandon said. "Look, I came to you guys without even knowing anything about this thousand dollars. But if you're gonna pay me for the information, I'm not gonna turn it down."

"How can we get in touch with you in the future? You have a cell phone?" Van asked.

"No, but I got a beeper," Brandon answered. "If you wanna get in touch with me, just beep me with the code, nine one one, and I'll know it's you guys. I'll go to a pay phone and call you back."

"Alright, well, what I need from you now is a statement," Tony explained. "Put everything in the statement that you can remember. Don't worry about spelling, just put it all down."

Van added, "When we come back, we'll have a photo array for you to view. Every picture has a number and you pick out the number of the person you saw leaving the building with the gun after the shooting."

Brandon agreed, and Tony and Van left him to write his statement in the interview room.

"Light," Van said, shaking his head. "Can you believe that?"

"Man, his name just keeps coming up," Tony added.

"You think this is another murder-for-hire?"

"I do," Tony said. "I think this was an order by Bulldog. I think his man, Light, took the hit because, like Donny said, Light probably had a problem with Carl selling in his area. Maybe he had to get permission from Bulldog to do the hit?"

"You know what, I kind of like that," said Van, nodding. "I think you may have something there. Bulldog gave him the okay to whack Carl 'cause he was interfering with his business."

"I'll go update the sergeant and you get the photo array together for Light."

"You got it."

After updating Detective Sergeant Richards about the case, Tony went to check out the photo array Van created. "The sergeant is advised and says to continue our course," Tony said to Van. "Let me see the photo array."

"It's the best I could do," Van apologized. "I couldn't find too many matches for his eyes. No one has eyes like that."

"Yeah, but it's pretty good," Tony said, nodding his head in approval after looking over Van's work. They both agreed it would work, and went back to the interview room to speak with Brandon.

"You finished with that statement?" Tony asked him.

"Yes, sir," he replied.

"It's pretty good," Tony complimented him after looking it over. "You have good handwriting. How far'd you go in school?"

"I went to college for two years. But I'm taking a break."

"What were you studying?" Van asked.

"Business," he answered.

"That's great," Tony said. "Don't give up, man. You need to get back into college."

"I will," Brandon said. "I'm gonna try."

"Okay," Tony said. "Don't just say that, though. You do it. Alright, now take a look at these photos. Look at all six and pick the number of the person who you saw with the gun. Circle his picture, then sign your name at the bottom."

Almost immediately, Brandon picked out Light. He circled the photo, then signed his name underneath.

"Great job, man," Tony said.

"So, what happens now?" Brandon asked.

"Well, for right now, nothing," Tony answered. "We have to get some paperwork together and make some moves. I'll be in touch, though. If you see Light, call nine one one. Tell 'em you see someone the police are looking for in a homicide. Then you call me. Here's my card."

"What about that money?" Brandon asked. "When do I get that?"

"You get the money after we make the arrest and you testify," Van explained. "But for now, we'll drop you off wherever you want to go."

"Can you just take me back to where you picked me up?"

"You want that to be our meeting place?" Tony asked.

"Yeah, that's a good place," Brandon confirmed.

They agreed to meet there in the future if anything came up, and headed out to the vehicle. When they reached it, Brandon took a widespread stance, leaned in to the car, and put his palms on the trunk.

"What are you doing, man?" asked Van.

"Don't you have to search me?"

Tony looked at Van and laughed. "Naw, man. We just do that the first time we meet someone we don't know. You're cool, man."

"Oh," Brandon said, his face flushing, and he got in the car.

They dropped him off at Castle Road and told him they would be in touch. When they got back to the house, they ordered Chinese food. Just after hanging up the phone, Detective Bradberry and Detective Ragland walked in.

"What's up, guys?" Detective Bradberry asked.

"Hey, guys," said Detective Ragland. "You guys need anything?"

"Not right now," Tony replied. "But in a couple of days, we may have a move on a possible perp for the homicide."

"Really?" asked Detective Bradberry.

"Yeah," Van confirmed. "We've got things shaking and moving over here."

"Sounds good," said Detective Ragland, and him and Detective Bradberry left.

As soon as Detectives Ragland and Bradberry left, Tony and Van discussed their next steps with Detective Sergeant Richards.

"So, what's the plan, guys?" she asked.

"First thing tomorrow," Tony started, "we go knock on mom's door to see if Light's home. If he is, we ask him to come in. If he's not, we interview mom and try to find out where he is."

"I'll ride with you guys, just in case he is there," she said.

"Sounds good," Van said. "Today we'll just finish with the DD5s on the witness and the photo array."

"Okay," she said, standing up from her seat. Tony and Van followed suit. "Thanks for lunch, guys. Back to work for me too. I've got some paperwork that needs my attention."

"As do we," said Tony, and they all headed to their respective desks to close out their day.

Chapter 14

After breakfast the next morning, they drove out to 2642 Tremont Avenue to try to talk to Jules Brown or his mother.

"What's his mom's name again?" asked Detective Sergeant Richards.

"Nina Brown," Tony answered.

They entered the building and took the elevator up to the seventh floor. Tony knocked on the door to apartment 7E.

"Who is it?" a female voice called out from inside.

"NYC police," Tony responded. "May we speak with you?"

"Police?" the woman repeated. The door opened.

"Good morning. I'm Detective Tony Richards, and this is my partner, Detective Van Morris," Tony said. He turned and gestured towards their boss and added, "And this is my supervisor, Detective Sergeant Sonia Richards."

"Good morning y'all," the woman greeted them. "What's this about?"

"May we come inside?" Tony asked.

"Sure. Come on in. Have a seat," she offered, and waved them inside the small, but clean apartment. In the living room was a love seat and a recliner. "Just grab a chair from the kitchen."

Tony walked into the kitchen and grabbed one of two tattered kitchen chairs. He placed it down in the living room next to Van and Detective Sergeant Richards, who were seated on the loveseat. Tony sat facing the woman, who was now seated in the recliner. "Are you Ms. Nina Brown?" he asked.

"Yes."

"We're here from the homicide squad and we're investigating the murder of one of your neighbors. Did you know a guy by the name of Carl White?"

"Carl White?" she repeated. "No, I don't think so. You say he was killed?"

"Yes," Tony confirmed. "He was shot inside the lobby of twenty-six thirty-eight Tremont. Do you live here alone?"

"Well, my son, Jules, sometimes stays here with me. But he mostly stays with a friend on the east side of town."

"And do you know that friend?" Tony asked.

"A woman named Lena Garcia. She lives over at the Park co-ops."

"Do you know her exact address?"

"I'll have to get that from my book," she said, rising from her chair. "Hold on a minute. I'll be right back."

She got up from the recliner and walked towards what appeared to be a bedroom at the back of the apartment. Detective Sergeant Richards leaned in to Tony and whispered, "You trying to get a promotion from third-grade? With all this information, she's just handing to you, you should easily be a second-grade detective."

"Are you putting in my recommendation?" Tony asked.

"Not just yet," Detective Sergeant Richards said, laughing. "I'm just saying."

"Okay, let me see, now," the woman said to herself as she came back into the living room, flipping through the pages of a small notebook. She sat back down in the recliner. "Here it is. Three zero five one Park Ave. Apartment nine D."

"Got it," Tony said, as he scrawled the address onto his notepad. "Do you have her phone number?"

"Oh, you know, I don't," she said, disappointed.

"That's okay," Tony assured her. "You've been very helpful. Are you expecting to see your son anytime soon?"

"Pssshh," she muttered and shook her head. "I don't ever know when that boy's coming 'round here. He just shows up whenever he wants."

"Well, if he does, will you please give him my card and tell him to give me a call?"

"Sure will," she agreed. "My son, he ain't in no trouble now is he?" "No we just want to speak to anyone who knew the victim."

"Okay, Ms. Brown," Tony said as he stood. "Thank you so much for speaking with us."

"It's been a pleasure," Detective Sergeant Richards added, and Van nodded in appreciation. "Take care, I'll give Jules the card if he shows up." "Thanks,"said Detective Richards.

When they got back to the vehicle, Detective Sergeant Richards said, "Let's take a ride over to

Park co-ops and see if he's hanging around the area."

"Sergeant," Van said. "You just took the words right out of my mouth."

They drove around the area of 3051 Park Avenue, but had no luck finding Jules. They decided to return another day with a larger group, and headed back to the office.

Back at the house, everyone hit the typewriters to complete their DD5s. After Tony finished, he called the United States Attorney's office.

"Hello, this is the U.S. Attorney's office, Ms. Ayesha Berry's line. Can I help you?"

"Hi, this is Detective Tony Richards, NYPD homicide squad," Tony replied. "May I speak with Ms. Berry, please?"

"Yes, of course. Hold on and I'll connect you."

Tony waited less than a minute before hearing another voice on the other end of the line. "U.S. Attorney Ayesha Berry speaking. How may I help you?"

"Hi, Ms. Berry. My name is Detective Tony Richards with the NYPD homicide squad. How are you?"

"I'm fine," she answered matter-of-factly. "How may I help you?"

"I have a homicide case in which I believe someone else ordered the perp to commit the crime. I think it might be a RICO case."

"Racketeer Influenced and Corrupt Organizations," she said in response. "Tell me about the case, briefly."

"I haven't arrested anyone yet. A couple of weeks ago, we got a call about a man shot in the Bronx. Four times in the head," Tony began. "His common law wife says she saw the shooter. We found out the victim sold cocaine in Harlem, an area that belongs to a guy named Ricardo Green, aka Bulldog. He runs the north part of Harlem's coke industry, and we have a witness who saw one of Bulldog's boys leaving the area of the homicide with a gun."

"This sounds like a very interesting case," Ms. Berry said. "What else do you know?"

"Well," Tony continued, "after further investigation, we found out from Captain Kahyle Ram of the North Narcotics division that they've been trying to get Bulldog for years. He seemed pretty sure that Bulldog has committed murder, but I guess he's got a high-paid lawyer on retention and a crew of three guys he grew up with who are real loyal to him. One of these guys is named Jules Brown. Goes by Light. He was spotted in the area of the crime and also used to sell in the same area as the victim. And we know Bulldog had words with the victim about infringing on his territory. I'd like to start a RICO case on him, if you think there could be anything there."

"I've met Captain Ram before at a conference meeting," Ms. Berry commented. "Now, how do you suggest we get this Bulldog if the captain says they've been trying for years?"

"I'm thinking we should just follow the money," Tony suggested. "If Bulldog has a hold on all the coke sold up in Harlem, he has to have left a money trail. If we follow his money – where he stashes it or how he launders it – maybe we can get him for laundering or tax evasion."

"Now that sounds good," Ms. Berry said. "I do know someone from the IRS investigative unit. We can get a financial background on him – I'll have him get on that right away. I do think we may have a case, so you keep doing what you're doing, and consider this a RICO case being investigated by my office."

"Sounds good," said Tony.

They shared contact information and agreed to stay in touch. Van walked back in the office just as Tony hung up the phone.

"We're on partner," Tony told him. "U.S. Attorney says we have a RICO case."

"Great!" Van exclaimed. "Are you gonna call the Bronx ADA's office?"

"You think I should?" Tony asked.

"Yeah," Van replied. "At least let them know that we're moving forward with this case."

"Okay. I'll call ADA Guevara and let her know what we have so far." Tony dialed the number to her office.

"Hello, ADA Stacy Guevara," she answered. "How can I help you?"

"Hi, Stacy. This is Tony, homicide squad."

"Hey, Tony," she replied cheerfully. "How have you been?"

"Fine. And you?"

"Great. How can I help you?"

"I just wanted to inform you that I'm investigating another homicide," Tony explained.

"We don't have the perp yet, but we do know who the perp is."

"Which homicide are you referring to?" she asked.

"Carl White," Tony answered. "Black male, shot in the head four times in the lobby of twenty-six thirty-eight Tremont."

"Hold on," she said. "Let me bring it up."

"It's another murder-for-hire case," Tony added. "But this time it's from another borough, and no money has been exchanged."

"Okay I've got it," she said. "So, what makes this a murder-for-hire if no money has been exchanged?"

"The hit was ordered by a big drug dealer from Harlem, and the guy responsible for the hit worked for him. I want to arrest them both," Tony explained. "I've already run this by U.S. Attorney Ayesha Berry."

"Okay," she answered sharply. "So why are you calling me?"

"Well, you were so good with the last homicide we worked on together, and I have a lot of respect for you," Tony explained. "But we've got a much better chance of getting this guy with a

RICO case than staying local, and no one has been able to touch him. I just didn't want you to hear about it from anyone else."

"Well, thank you, Detective," she said. "It's nice to hear from people who care. And I do know that you care, even if I would have rather handled this case out of my office."

"It's no problem," Tony said.

"If you think you can get this guy for murder one, then I'll just say good luck to you. And if there's anything I can help you with, don't be afraid to call."

"Thank you," Tony replied, and hung up the phone. He called out to Van, "Hey, I just spoke with Stacy. She sounded a little pissed that we're going through the U.S. Attorney's office, but seems to understand."

"That's good, right?" Van asked.

"Yeah, I guess so. I just feel better having told her up front."

Detectives Bradberry and Ragland walked in.

"How you guys doing?" Detective Bradberry asked. "Working hard as usual?"

"Yeah," Tony answered. "You know how it goes. Hey, listen. Are you guys available to help us with this case tomorrow?"

"Sure, what do you need?" Detective Bradberry replied.

"Tomorrow we're going hunting for Light," Tony explained. "We believe he's shacking up with this broad named Lena Garcia. You may want to get caught up by reading the case files."

Detective Ragland spoke up. "Who are we going with?"

"You two, me, Van, and the sergeant," Tony answered. "Just for a show of force."

Detective Bradberry said, "I think that's more than enough. What time are we gonna do this?"

"First thing in the morning, before breakfast," Tony said.

"What?" Van interjected. "We gotta have breakfast first, *before* we go out."

"Listen, I wanna get this guy early, before he has breakfast," Tony replied.

"Well, if we *don't* get him, then breakfast is on *you*," Van asserted.

"What is this a bet, or something?"

"No," Van said, pretending to be annoyed. "Just you have to buy breakfast if we don't get Light in the morning."

"Breakfast sounds good to me," said Detective Bradberry.

"Alright, alright," Tony agreed. "I'll get breakfast if he's not there, okay? Happy?"

"Sounds like a plan," Detective Ragland said.

"Here's the case folder," Tony said, handing over a heavy stack of files. "Make sure you guys catch up."

Detectives Bradberry and Ragland sat down with the folder and started reading, while Tony and Van finished their DD5s. When Tony was done, he went to the sergeant's office to tell her about his conversation with the U.S. Attorney's office, and they discussed what time to leave to go hunting for Light in the morning.

Tony returned to the office and confirmed the time with everyone as they finished their reading and paperwork and started packing up to leave for the day.

"Don't forget to dress down tomorrow," Tony reminded everyone, and they all headed home.

Chapter 15

By the time everyone got to the office in the morning, Tony had all the radios assigned and the car keys set up. Detective Sergeant Richards came in as he was reviewing the homicide folder with Detectives Bradberry and Ragland.

"Is everyone ready to roll?" asked Detective Sergeant Richards.

"Yeah. Let's do this," said Tony, and they all picked up their radios.

"I'll ride with you guys," Detective Sergeant Richards said to Tony and Van, and they headed out.

When they arrived at 3051 Park Avenue, they took the elevator to the ninth floor. They got out of the elevator and Detective Sergeant Richards said, "I'll stand back. You two lead." She motioned with her chin at Tony and Van. Tony found the door labeled 9D and knocked on the door.

"Who is it?" a muffled female voice asked from inside the apartment.

"NYPD Detectives," Tony answered. "Can you open the door so we can speak with you?"

"What do you want?" the woman asked again, much more clearly, and it was obvious she was standing just on the other side of the door.

"We'd like to speak with you, but not through the door," Tony said. "Can you please open the door?"

After a few moments of silence, the door creaked open and a woman peered out into the hallway. "Yes?" she asked, in a tone equally suspicious and annoyed.

"Hi," Tony said. "I'm Detective Tony Richards and this is my partner, Detective Van Morris. There are a couple other detectives with us, and also my supervisor, Detective Sergeant Sonia Richards."

"What do you want?" the woman asked abruptly.

"We would like to speak with you, but not in the hallway. We don't want your neighbors to hear us. Can we come inside?"

"It's not clean."

"To be honest," Tony replied, "my apartment could use a cleaning right now too. And we'll only be a couple of minutes. We're not worried about clean."

"Come on in, I guess," she conceded. She opened the door the rest of the way, and they walked into the apartment. "Have a seat."

"That won't be necessary," Tony said. "We only need a couple of minutes. May I have your name, please?"

"Lena Garcia," she answered.

"Ms. Garcia," Tony started, "are you here alone? Or is there someone else here with you?"

"I'm here alone. There isn't anyone else here with me."

"Do you know a male by the name of Jules Brown, or Light?"

"No, I never heard that name before," she answered. "What's this about?"

"Well, I'm a homicide detective and we're looking for Mr. Brown."

"Why you looking for him here?" she asked defensively.

"We've been told that he stays here sometimes."

"Who told you that?"

"If he does stay here anytime soon, I'd like for you to give him my card the next time that you see him."

"Listen," Ms. Garcia said, annoyed. "I don't know him. And I'm not giving your card to someone I don't know, alright?"

"Is it alright if we look around?" Van asked.

"Go ahead, look," she said from the corner of her mouth. "You won't find no one."

Tony noticed two bowls and two glasses on the kitchen table. He took out his notepad and said, "Could you just sign here that we have your permission to search your apartment?"

Just as she took the pen and signed her name, a loud thump came from a room at the back of the apartment.

"What was that?" asked Tony.

Ms. Garcia shrugged and said, "I didn't hear anything."

"Here's what we're going to do. You two," Detective Sergeant Richards said, pointing to Detective Ragland and Detective Bradberry, "stay out here with Miss Garcia. The three of us will go check out that noise. Is that your bedroom?"

"Yeah," Ms. Garcia answered.

Detective Sergeant Richards, Tony, and Van all drew their weapons and moved slowly through the apartment. The living room was small and furnished with an old loveseat and a mismatched chair, and there were two other doors between the living room and the bedroom. After checking inside each, a closet and a bathroom, they approached the bedroom door.

Detective Sergeant Richards took the lead with Tony and Van following close behind. She knocked on the door, but got no response. She stepped to one side of the door while Tony crossed to stand on the other side, and she slowly turned the door knob. The three detectives slowly entered the bedroom, pointing their guns in each direction they stepped. A soft, muffled sound came from a closet on the far side of the room. Detective Sergeant Richards motioned for Tony to guard the right side of the closet, and for Van to take the left side. She positioned herself directly in front of the door.

"This is the police," she said. "Open the closet door slowly, and let me see your hands." The stillness in the room was palpable. The door remained closed. Detective Sergeant Richards repeated, "This is the police. Come out of the closet with your hands first, and move slowly."

Suddenly, the door flung open. Several gunshots were fired. Detective Sergeant Richards was struck in the chest as Light came flying out of the closet. Van fired his weapon, striking Light once in his right shoulder. Tony fired just a moment later, striking Light in the left side of his body, causing him to drop his gun and fall to the ground.

Detective Sergeant Richards fell to the ground as well, and Detectives Bradberry and Ragland burst into the bedroom with weapons drawn. Tony and Van were already placing handcuffs on Light and Tony took out his radio and called Central.

"Homicide squad to central with an emergency message, kay," he breathed into his radio.

"Go with your message, kay," came the immediate response.

"We have an MOS shot at thirty fifty-one Park Ave, nine D," Tony reported. "We also have a male down and in custody. We need two busses, a patrol supervisor, crime scene and additional units. Put a rush on the busses, kay."

"Ten four," the operator answered. "Member of service down and suspect in custody. Sending additional units, kay."

Detective Sergeant Richards was trying to catch her breath as the gunshot had knocked the wind out of her. Tony reached out and removed her weapon from her hand. "Help is on the way," he assured her. "Just breathe and try to relax."

"What can we do?" Detective Ragland asked.

"Grab some towels from the bathroom and bring them here," Van answered.

Detective Ragland ran into the bathroom and grabbed several towels. He passed a few of them to Van and he applied them to Detective Sergeant Richards' wounds. Detective Ragland did the same for Light. He was breathing rapidly, and a pool of blood started to form around him.

"Calm down, Light," Van instructed as he continued to hold pressure to his boss' wounds. "You're gonna hyperventilate. Slow down your breathing."

"Sergeant, you alright?" Tony asked Detective Sergeant Richards. She nodded, but didn't speak. "Don't move. Just try to breathe. Let me get this vest off of you."

Tony unstrapped her vest and carefully removed it. A bullet fragment had lodged inside the vest, and she had a small drop of blood seeping through her shirt.

"Okay, Sergeant," Tony said. "Just sit still. A bus is on the way."

Tony placed her gun back inside her holster, and two minutes later there was a loud banging on the door.

"I'll get it," Detective Bradberry volunteered, and when she opened the door, Officers Robinson and Williams came into the apartment.

"Is everyone okay?" asked Officer Robinson.

"Yeah," Detective Bradberry said. "We have a perp shot, and the sergeant got shot too."

"What do you need us to do?" Officer Williams asked.

"Set up a crime scene in the hallway and don't let anyone in except EMS, the supervisor, and Crime Scene. Take your notepad and get the names of everyone entering the building."

"Excuse me, please. EMS!" someone announced loudly from the front of the apartment. "I need to get in here. You have someone shot, right?"

"In the bedroom," Tony called out in response, and the EMS guys appeared at the bedroom door. "Over here first. My boss got shot. One to the chest."

The EMS officers knelt beside Detective Sergeant Richards. "Hey, Sergeant. How you doing? Can you talk?"

"Yeah," she said. "I can talk." Her voice was hoarse from the impact of the round to her chest.

"I need to get to your wound and get your vitals," the EMS officer told her. He took out a blood pressure pad and placed it around her left arm. Another EMS officer undid the buttons on her shirt and exposed a small laceration and a large bruise on her chest.

"Tell me if you feel this?" he said as he touched the bruise. Detective Sergeant Richards winced and nodded. "Okay, good. I don't feel any broken bones, but you do have a nasty bruise and you may wind up with a small scar where the blood is coming from. We'd like to take you to the hospital for overnight observation. But you're gonna be just fine."

Relief washed over her face and smiles spread across the faces of Tony and Van, who was still holding onto Light.

Another EMS officer appeared in the doorway and said, "Is someone in here shot?"

The first two officers nodded and gestured towards Light, and then carried Detective Sergeant Richards out of the room.

"I'll ride in the bus with the sergeant and get the info from EMS when we get to Jacobi Hospital," Detective Bradberry offered.

"Great," said Tony, and he picked up Light's weapon with a cotton shirt that had been on the bed.

Two additional EMS officers came into the room and started to work on Light. "We have to take the cuffs off him for now so we can treat him," one of the officers said.

Van bent down and uncuffed Light, and the EMS officers started to work on him. His breathing had become shallow and after they patched up his open wounds, they decided to rush him to the hospital.

"We're gonna lift him by his arms and legs and place him on the stretcher in the hallway. You ready?" one of the EMS officers announced.

They lifted Light up and carried him onto the stretcher. Officer Robinson came into the room and said, "Sergeant Juan Santos, the patrol supervisor, told me to escort the perp to the hospital."

"That's okay," Tony said. "Detective Ragland will escort him. Thanks, though. Just keep taking good notes."

"You got it," Officer Robinson said, and Detective Ragland left with the EMS workers to rush Jules to Jacobi Hospital.

"Hey, partner," Van said, sitting back against the wall and exhaling sharply. "You okay?"

"I'm fine," Tony answered. "You?'"

"I'm good," Van said, nodding. "But we have a lot of paperwork to do."

"Yeah, I know."

"Hey, detectives," said another officer that had just walked in. It was the patrol supervisor, Sergeant Santos. "I wasn't trying to run your show by trying to send my guy with the perp. I didn't know you had another detective here in the room with you."

"Don't worry about it, Sergeant," Tony replied. "We just need to keep control of our incidents. Detective Ragland was already here, so he just went to keep the consistency with the case."

A few minutes later, Detective Ryan Riggs walked into the bedroom.

"We have got to stop meeting like this, guys," he said, extending his hand towards Van. Van stood and shook his hand and Tony did the same.

"So, what do we have?" Detective Riggs asked.

"Our Sergeant got shot and we both shot the perp," Tony explained. "The perp's gun is on the bed. We have our weapons and the Sergeant still has hers. She didn't fire hers."

"I'm gonna need both of your weapons for ballistics checks," Detective Riggs announced. "You guys have backups, right?" They confirmed that they did and Detective Riggs collected their guns. He placed them on the bed next to crime scene evidence bags and said, "Alright, I need to have the room, guys."

Tony and Van walked out into the living room and sat down, Tony on the chair and Van on the couch. The patrol supervisor emerged from the kitchen

"Sergeant Juan," Tony said, "did you send Ms. Garcia to the house?"

"Yeah," he replied. "She was transported there by patrol. Who's catching on this one?"

"Detective Tony Richards, Homicide Squad, shield one two three," Tony answered.

"Alright. I'll put a man on the door until Crime Scene finishes and then seal the apartment"

"Thanks, sir," Van said. "See you back at the house. We're out, and thanks for your quick response."

"Just doing our job," Sergeant Juan replied.

Tony and Van arrived back at the house to a barrage of officers clapping and hooting. They were given high fives and pats on their backs as they walked through the office. Sergeant Blackwell was serving as the acting sergeant while Detective Sergeant Richards was out on leave of absence, and he also greeted the men with a loud round of applause.

"I'm proud to know you guys," he said. "You saved Sonia's life and took down the perp. Well done."

They smiled, headed into the office, and sat down at their desks. They had just started their paperwork when Sergeant Blackwell walked over to Tony's desk. "What do you want us to do with Ms. Lena Garcia?" he asked.

"You can give her a ride back home," Tony said. "Tell her she can remove the seal on her apartment and that we aren't gonna charge her."

"You're letting her go?" the sergeant asked.

"Yeah, she didn't do anything," Tony answered. "She wasn't wanted for anything when we first got to her apartment and we can't hold her for lying. Just let her go home."

"Alright," Sergeant Blackwell replied. "If you say so. I'll get patrol to drop her home."

Tony and Van started on the pile of paperwork that awaited them. They had to fill out firearm discharge forms and DD5s. About three hours into filling out these forms, Detective Bradberry walked into the office. "What's up guys?"

"How's the sergeant?" asked Tony.

"She's resting in Jacobi Hospital," she answered. "They gave her an IV and told her to stay awake for the first two hours, but now she's trying to get some sleep. She has blunt trauma, and a stitch and they said she would just be there overnight for observation."

"Great," said Van.

"Thanks for all your help, Kay," Tony said. "You and Dee are great workers and we're so glad you were there with us."

"And I'm glad you guys were there," she said. "You saved the sergeant's life and took down the perp. I'm really glad we joined your team."

Van and Tony both thanked her and she sat down in the office to begin her paperwork while they continued theirs. Two hours later, Detective Ragland showed up.

"Hey, Dee," said Detective Bradberry.

"Hey, everybody," Detective Ragland announced. "Great job, guys! You two are the talk of the town. I even heard that the mayor visited the hospital to see Sergeant Sonia, and had a lot of good things to say about the two detectives who saved her life."

"Really?" said Tony, surprised.

"Yeah. He said you should get an award for your *fine work*."

"For real?" Van replied.

"Yeah," confirmed Detective Ragland. "I heard him talking to the Chief of Detectives at the hospital. Anyway, Light is out of surgery, unconscious, but in stable condition and he's still being held in ICU. He's under arrest but not charged officially. Patrol is guarding him. He should be able to talk in a couple days."

"Thanks, Dee," Tony said. "You guys are strong together, especially under fire. We appreciate that you two are with us and are truly a part of our family."

Detective Ragland joined in on the paperwork session and Officers Robinson and Williams showed up to drop off their reports.

"Man, this is the most paperwork I've seen in a long time," Tony kidded as Officer Robinson handed his over. "But seriously, great job, guys. Thanks for your quick response to assist us and for all your help."

"You guys need anything else?" Officer Robinson asked. "Like something to eat? Our treat."

"If you're treatin', then I'm eatin'," said Van.

"You got a problem, man," Tony said, and they all laughed. Officer Williams took everyone's orders and promised to be back shortly.

Half an hour later, they returned with the food and all sat down around the table in the break room for lunch.

"What's next on your list?" Detective Bradberry asked.

"We're off the next two, which is a good thing," Tony said. "But when we get back, we'll see where Light is at. If we can speak with him, we'll interview him and see where that leads. If we can talk to Light, I think we can get him to flip on Bulldog. We'll also have to go to Psychology to get our guns back."

"What if he doesn't flip?" asked Detective Ragland. "What are you gonna do about Bulldog?"

"I don't know yet, but I'm not gonna leave him alone."

They finished eating, completed their paperwork, and agreed to discuss their plans further when they got back to the office in two days.

Chapter 16

After two days off, they all felt refreshed returning to work. Sergeant Blackwell stopped by their desks first thing on the morning of their return.

"Good morning, detectives," he said. "Sonia's doing fine and should be back in the office by the end of the week. If anyone needs anything, though, please come talk to me. My door is always open. Let's have a safe tour."

Van and Tony had an appointment with Psychology. It was customary after every shooting for all officers involved to be cleared by the psych doctor to get any weapons back and return to active duty. They hopped in the car together and headed downtown for the visit.

An hour later, after Tony had been cleared, Van came out of the doctor's office and gave Tony a thumbs up. "We're back," Van said. "Let's go pick up our weapons and check on the ballistics for Light's weapon."

At the evidence lab, they met up again with Detective Ryan Riggs.

"Good morning, detectives," Detective Riggs greeted them. "How's it going?"

"Ready to get our guns back," Tony said, grinning. "Got our certificates from the psych doctor."

Detective Riggs laughed. "I know it," he said teasingly. "I see you cops all the time. Can't wait to get those weapons back. Come on into my office and we'll get you two suited back up."

They walked towards the back of the warehouse and went into his lab.

"Wow, this is some lab," said Tony.

"Yeah. We have every gun ever used and confiscated here. It's somewhat of a museum. Here's yours," said Detective Riggs, handing over Tony's gun. "And here, Van. Here's yours."

"Thanks, man," Tony said. "What did you find out about Light's weapon?"

"Well," he started, "the weapon possessed by Jules Brown, aka Light, was most certainly the weapon used to kill your victim from twenty-six thirty-eight Tremont."

"Good job, Ryan," said Van. "Any other bodies to add to it?"

"No," answered Detective Riggs. "No other matches. Just that one for now. But if you do get any other bodies, I'll do a comparison check.

If we get any more matches, he'll go down for those as well."

"We're going to talk to him today at the hospital," Tony said.

"How's the sergeant doing? Is she home?"

"Yeah," Tony answered. "She's fine. Should be returning at the end of the week. We gotta run, though. Thanks again, Ryan. You take care, okay."

"See ya, man," Van added.

"Alright, guys," Detective Riggs said. "You take care and good hunting."

Tony and Van walked out of the evidence warehouse with their firearms back on their hips. They decided to call Detective Sergeant Richards to see how she was feeling.

They put her on speaker so they could both talk to her. She was in good spirits and thanked them both for saving her life. They filled her in on the confirmation they received on Light's weapon being the murder weapon, and on their plan to visit him at Jacobi Hospital and then inform the U.S. Attorney's office as well.

"Okay, partner," Van said when they hung up with the sergeant. "To Jacobi?"

"You got it."

They arrived at Jacobi hospital and went straight up to ICU. A police officer was sitting in front of the door to the unit.

"Hey, I'm Detective Richards," Tony introduced himself as he showed his badge. "And this is my partner, Detective Morris. We're the assigned detectives to this case."

"Yeah, I recognize you guys," he said. "Good job the other night."

"Thanks," Tony answered. "Why don't you go get something to eat until we're done interviewing him. We should be done in an hour."

"Okay," he agreed. "Be back in an hour".

Tony and Van entered the intensive care unit and then Light's room, which was just inside the hallway. Light's eyes were closed and his arm was in a sling. He was lying in the only bed in the room.

"Hey, Mr. Brown," Tony greeted him. "I'm Detective Tony Richards and this is my partner, Detective Van Morris. Do you know where you are?"

Light nodded, almost imperceptibly.

"Are you able to speak?" Tony asked.

"I can speak," Light answered abruptly and with a raspy voice.

"Do you know why you're here?"

"Yeah. I got shot."

"Who shot you?"

"Man, I don't know," he answered, again clearly agitated. "What do you want?"

"Well, I'd like to explain to you everything we know, and then if you sign this Miranda warning sheet, we'll listen to whatever it is that you know."

"Okay," Light said, sounding suspicious.

"We're with the homicide squad and we're investigating a murder at twenty-six thirty-eight Tremont Avenue," Tony said. He searched Light's face for a reaction, but saw none. "A black male by the name of Carl White was shot four times in the head. Two witnesses have identified you as the person responsible for his death, and we know you were staying at thirty fifty-one Park Avenue. My sergeant and I, and three other detectives, went there looking for you. Ms. Garcia tried to tell us she was home alone, but we heard a noise from inside the bedroom and you jumped out of the closet, firing. When you shot my supervisor, my partner and I returned fire and struck you, and landed you here in Jacobi Hospital."

"So, you two shot me?" he asked, wide-eyed.

"Yes," Tony replied, matter-of-factly. "And like I told you before, you'll have to sign this Miranda if you want to discuss this further."

"Well, then, you may as well leave, cause I ain't signing no Miranda."

"That's fine," Tony stated, turning towards the door. "We'll just charge you with murder, attempted murder of a police officer, possession of a weapon, firing a weapon inside city limits, resisting–"

"Okay, okay," yelled Light. "I get it, I get it. You'll put me away forever."

"No," Van interjected. "It's actually worse than that. Heard of the electric chair? The State of New York still has the death penalty, you know."

"The death penalty?" Light asked in disbelief.

"You shot and killed Carl White," Tony said. "You shot my sergeant. You discharged a weapon within city limits. You unlawfully possessed a weapon. You resisted arrest. So, yes. The death penalty. Unless – hey, you like fishing?"

"Fishing?" Light asked.

"Yeah," Tony confirmed. He gestured as if he were casting a fishing line and whistled as he pretended to reel it in. "Fishing."

"Man, whatchyu talkin' about?"

"Well, when you go fishing and you catch a little fish, you throw it back in the water because you wanna catch a bigger fish," Tony explained. "Do you know any bigger fishes?"

"Man, you want me to rat?" Light exclaimed.

"I want you to save your own life," Tony clarified. "But if you'd rather take your chances, then that's up to you."

Light was quiet for a moment. Then he asked, "Can you protect me? I mean, not just out here, but in jail?"

"Before we get into all that, let me read you your Miranda. Then we can talk."

"Fine," Light conceded. "Go ahead."

Tony read him his rights and he agreed to talk to them without an attorney present. With his arm in a sling, Light signed the sheet Van gave him to document his agreement.

"Who do you work for?" Tony asked him.

"First tell me how you're gonna protect me," demanded Light. "If I go to jail, they'll still get me. So how you gonna protect me?"

"Witness protection," Tony answered.

"Are you kidding me?" Light scoffed. "Witness protection means I gotta leave the city. No way."

"Listen to me," Tony started, "witness protection has never loss a client. Once you go into witness protection, if you follow the rules, you'll be protected the rest of your life. But you have to leave the city to start over. You and your mother will have the best protection they can offer."

"Why you mention my mother? You know her?"

"Yes. We met her three days ago. Do you love her? Care about her?" Tony asked, one eyebrow raised.

"'Course I love my mama," Light answered through clenched teeth.

"Well, if we found her, don't you think your boss can? Or may already have?"

Light was quiet again for a few moments. "You could protect my mama if I speak to you?"

"We could get her into protective custody if she agreed to leave the city," Tony confirmed. "Then you could both live a happy life in another state."

"If you promise to get my mama outta New York, then I'll help you."

"You got a deal," Tony said. "Now, who's your boss?"

"Real name's Ricardo Green," Light answered without hesitation this time. "They call him Bulldog. He runs the north side of the Harlem coke industry. He lives in Sugar Hill and drives a gold Benz." Light stopped talking, folded his arms across his chest, and turned his face away from the detectives.

"Keep going," Tony prompted.

"Man, you asked who he was," Light answered as he turned, red-faced, back towards Tony and Van. "I told you who he was."

"Tell us more," Van added with a forced smile.

Light sighed heavily. "He's twenty-two, black Hispanic. I'm one of his three lieutenants, plus Seven and Kool. Growing up, we were boys, and always got into trouble. We even went to juvy together."

"Seven and Kool?" Tony asked.

"Jason Rite and Zak Black," Light clarified, turning his face away from the detectives again. "They both still live on Eighth. I did shoot Carl because Carl was stupid. I've known Carl for years. Since we were kids."

"So how did you all young men get yourself into this business?"

"Bulldog used to go up to Washington Heights and cop," Light began. "One day, he went inside this apartment and they were speaking Spanish. They figured he didn't know what they were saying because he looks black. But he did know. He heard 'em say another guy was coming up the block in ten minutes with two keys of coke. So, Bulldog comes back outside and tells us we gotta run this guy for the coke. So, the guy comes walking by and we took him. Knocked him out. Obviously, he never showed up to the apartment with the two keys of coke they expected.

"The next day, Bulldog goes back up to that apartment and tells the guy he knows where his missing coke is. The guy offers him a hundred dollars to get it back. Bulldog tells him he doesn't want his money this time, but that he wants to work for him. So, the guy says bring me those two keys of coke and we'll talk. Half hour later, Bulldog goes back with the coke and that's it. They start doing business."

"So, who's this guy that Bulldog worked for?" Tony asked.

Light shrugged his shoulders. "We never met the guy," he said. "Bulldog wouldn't say. He just showed up with the coke when we ran out. The reason Bulldog ordered the hit on Carl is Carl wouldn't step off. I told Carl that Bulldog was hitting that spot for years and he couldn't just move in without asking. But Carl told me to take a hike. Said Bulldog didn't own the world and he just kept selling. Stupid."

"How did Carl get people to buy from him if Bulldog ran that part of town for so long?" Van asked.

"Carl cut the price down by two dollars," Light explained. "Word got back to Bulldog and he just said Carl had to go. Bulldog doesn't let no one try him, and he said if I didn't take Carl out, that maybe I was getting soft. Then he started talking about all the bodies that he had under his belt. Said he took 'em all out with his gold nine, and that nobody could even find them. Like he was threatening me. So, I agreed to take him out."

"Where are these bodies?" Tony asked.

"That's my insurance," Light answered smugly. "I'll tell you that when you arrest Bulldog?"

"And what will we arrest Bulldog for?" Tony asked, tilting his head.

"What you mean?" Light exclaimed. "I just told you he killed people. I told you he sells drugs. Ain't that enough?"

"To be honest with you," Tony said, "it's not enough. All we've got is your word against his. And he has big time lawyers, so without evidence, we can't arrest him."

"So, he's gonna get away with all that?"

"Unless we can find those bodies," Van offered. "And prove that Bulldog shot them. Your testimony helps, but we need proof. Capiche?"

"Yeah."

"If we find those bodies," Tony said, "then Bulldog will never see light again."

Two minutes went by without any of them speaking a word. Finally, Light said, "Alright. I'll tell you where they are. You ever heard of Harem projects?"

Light explained, in detail, the alleged location of the bodies in a series of connected underground tunnels that ran throughout the city. He also detailed how they disposed of the bodies and used lime power so the odor wouldn't spread. Finally, he offered to take Tony and Van to the bodies himself.

"So, my time in jail," he said, "how much time I gotta do now that I'm helping you?"

"That isn't up to me," Tony answered. "I have to present this to the U.S. Attorney and see what she thinks. She'll get someone over here to do an interview with you on video. You just repeat everything you just told us, and then we take it from there."

"I gotta trust you Detective Richards," Light said. "My life and my mama's life is in your hands."

"Thanks for coming clean with us," said Tony. "I'm gonna set up a search for those bodies with patrol and we'll talk to you later. Get some rest."

Tony and Van walked out of ICU and found the assigned police officer sitting just outside the room.

"Take care, officer," Tony said. "Don't forget, he's under arrest. So, no visitors, except law enforcement and keep that visitor's log up for us."

"Got it, detectives," he answered, saluting them as they left.

"I've never heard of Harem projects having a tunnel that leads to the city, you?" Tony asked Van as they walked back to the car.

"Nah," Van agreed. "First I've heard of that, Tony."

When they got back to the house, Tony advised Sergeant Blackwell of the information they had gotten from Light. Sergeant Blackwell said he would contact Emergency Services to get a DOA smelling dog and some extra officers to assist with the search. Tony agreed to get the crime scene units, digging equipment, EMS units to confirm the DOAs, and the ME units to carry out the bodies.

Tony also agreed to contact the news to get them to hold off on the story so Bulldog and his crew didn't have time to leave the city. Sergeant Blackwell suggested Tony tell the news that the bodies were found by a neighborhood kid so Bulldog would be much less likely to be spooked into leaving once the story did get out.

Van and Tony split the call list of departments they needed help from, and Tony's final call was to U.S. Attorney Ayesha Berry. She congratulated them on the collar and said she and her investigator were on their way to Jacobi Hospital to interview Light. Tony told her that he and Van would meet her there.

"Let's leave in fifteen, okay?" Tony said to Van.

"Sounds good," Van replied, and in just ten minutes, they were off to the hospital.

When they arrived, the same officer was still sitting in front of ICU.

"Hey, officer," Tony greeted him. "Any changes since we left?"

"None," he answered, and Tony and Van walked into the room to speak to Light.

Tony explained to Light that the U.S. Attorney was on her way and would answer whatever questions he had that Tony and Van couldn't answer. They waited just ten minutes for her to arrive.

"Gentleman," she collectively greeted everyone. "I'm U.S. Attorney Ayesha Berry, and this is my investigator, Vinnie Morg." They all shook hands before Ms. Berry turned her full attention to Light.

"You must be Mr. Brown," she said.

"Yes, ma'am," Light replied.

"Are you feeling okay, today, Mr. Brown?"

"Yes."

"I understand from Detective Richards that you've been advised of your rights and you're willing to speak with me regarding the homicide of Mr. Carl White. And you're willing to share information regarding Mr.Ricardo Green, is that right?"

"Yes," he answered, looking defeated.

A man appeared in the doorway carrying a large black duffel bag. Ms. Berry smiled at him and turned back to Light.

"This is my videographer, Chris," Ms. Berry announced. "He's going to set up video for the interview, and then you can tell us everything you know."

The videographer took just a few minutes to set up and Ms. Berry immediately began the interview. Light shared everything that he had shared with Tony and Van, and the interview was over in about twenty minutes. Chris broke down his equipment and left as quickly as he had arrived.

"So how much time you think I'm looking at?" Light asked the U.S. Attorney.

"It's hard to say," she answered. "It all depends on how well we do with the arrest of Bulldog and whatever we find in the catacombs. Right now, I'd say you're looking at seventy-five years to life."

Light's jaw dropped. "After all I gave you?" he exclaimed defiantly as he bolted upright in his hospital bed. "Seventy-five to life. You *must* be kidding me!"

"Actually, sir," Ms. Berry said sternly, glaring at Light. "With your offenses, it could be much worse. But like I said, it depends on the findings. Remember, this isn't state time. This is federal. There is no plea bargaining, so let's just see what happens."

She stood and shook Light's hand, which he offered reluctantly. "We'll be in touch," she said, and walked away to address Tony and Van, who had positioned themselves in the doorway.

"When are you guys doing the catacombs?"

"Later today," Tony answered. "We wanna get this done as soon as possible."

"Good. Keep me posted."

Tony and Van grabbed lunch on the way back to the house. As soon as they arrived at the office, Sergeant Blackwell shouted across the room, "Everything's a go on my side. What time should we be set to roll out?

"Two hours, tops," Tony answered. "I just gotta make a few phone calls."

Two hours went by and Sergeant Blackwell appeared at Tony's desk. "You guys ready to head out?"

"Yeah," said Tony. "Who you riding with? Us, or Kay and Dee?"

"I'm riding with the stars, of course," he said, laughing. "I've never made the news, so I'm hoping today will be my debut."

They all laughed and headed out to the Harem projects. A slew of law enforcement from multiple divisions were there waiting, and Tony addressed the group.

"In a few minutes, we're gonna descend into the tombs," he stated. "We'll follow the lead of the cadaver dogs. Stay close together and wait for the command to move before doing anything. Good hunting."

The officers with the dogs lead the way into the tunnels. Inside, it was almost pitch black and a strange odor surrounded them as the dogs simultaneously came to an abrupt stop and started to wag their tails.

"We have a hit," one of the officers called out to the group.

Tony ordered those with shovels to start digging, and called in some spotlights and the EMS guys to examine any bodies they might find. Van took notes and Detective Ragland had the video recorder to capture the find. Ten minutes into the digging, a body was found.

"We got one!" an EMS officer called out.

"Number two, right here," another officer shouted.

"Numbers three and four!"

A foul odor was now permeating the air all around them. The medical examiner took the four bodies and placed each in a body bag.

"I'll take them to the coroner's office and examine them," he said, and his assistants zipped up the bags and removed the bodies. Everyone packed up their equipment and left the underground site. When they emerged, the news crews were waiting for them.

"I have a statement to make," Tony said, raising his hand and addressing the small crowd. "My name is Detective Tony Richards, and I'm with the Bronx homicide squad. This site is now an official crime scene. No one may enter the premises. We have discovered the skeletal remains of several bodies, and this is an active investigation. If you have any further questions, please refer them to our public relations department."

He walked away as the reporters shouted questions at him. He ignored them and walked straight to the car with Van and Sergeant Blackwell. They drove off as quickly as they could.

"Good job, Tony!" Sergeant Blackwell congratulated him. "You handled that very well and I am proud to know you. Can I get your autograph?" They all laughed at that and discussed the details of the find on the way back to the house. As soon as they arrived, Tony called the U.S. Attorney's office.

"Hello," a woman's voice answered on the other end of the line. "U.S. Attorney Ayesha Berry, how can I help you?"

"Hi, Ms. Berry. This is Detective Tony Richards."

"How did it go?"

"Real well," he replied. "We recovered four bodies, all skeletal. The ME, Mr. West, said he'd examine the bodies at the lab and inform us of his findings."

"Great," she said. "So, Light was telling the truth."

"It appears so."

"When can you and your partner come back to my office?"

"We could make it over there tomorrow," Tony answered, looking at Van with his eyebrows raised as he spoke. Van nodded in agreement.

"That'll be fine. Come on over tomorrow and we'll go from there."

Tony got started on his paperwork as soon as he hung up the phone. Van, Detective Bradberry, and Detective Ragland had already started working on theirs.

"Where's my typewriter?" asked Sergeant Blackwell.

"You don't have to type, Sergeant," Tony said. "We'll take care of it."

"No, no," he said, shaking his head emphatically. "I spoke to patrol. I spoke to

Emergency Services, so I'll type my share of DD5s."

When they were all done with their respective paperwork, Tony said, "Hey guys, listen. I just want to thank each of you for all the help you've given me so far. Without you guys, I wouldn't have ever gotten this far."

"So, what you're saying is, breakfast is on you tomorrow, right?" Everyone laughed and Tony lightly punched Van in the shoulder in jest.

"You got it," Tony agreed. "One donut a piece."

"Hey," Sergeant Blackwell said, laughing, "a donut's a donut!"

"No, but seriously," Tony said. "Breakfast is definitely on me tomorrow."

Chapter 17

The next morning, Tony walked into the homicide office with a bag filled with bagels, cream cheese, butter, and jelly. He also had a large boxed coffee with containers of cream and packets of sugar. He set everything down on a large table near the center of all the desks.

"Breakfast!" he shouted across the office. "You better come and get it." Everyone looked up and immediately started moving towards the food.

"Thanks, Tony," said Van, the first to get in line.

"Yeah, eat up," Tony said with a grin. "'Cause this is the last time I'm buying."

After eating, Tony called the medical examiner, Mr. West, to discuss the causes of death of the bodies they had found the previous day. Armed with that information, he called the U.S. Attorney's office.

"Hello? U.S. Attorney Ayesha Berry speaking," she answered. "How can I help you?"

"Good morning, Ms. Berry," Tony greeted her. "This is Detective Richards, again. How are you?"

"Good morning, Detective Richards. I'm doing fine. Are you and your partner still planning on seeing me this morning?"

"Oh, yes. I was just calling to give you a heads up about the bodies we found last night."

"Go on," she said.

"The medical examiner, Mr. West, found that all victims had one head shot from a large caliber round. He said the grooves in their skulls have the same centrifugal shape, and were all caused by the same caliber weapon. He thinks they all took head shots from the same gun and I believe that gun belongs to Bulldog."

"Do you know what type of gun he carries?"

"Light says it's a gold nine millimeter, and we've gotten similar information from others."

"We've got to get this Bulldog. What time are you and Detective Morris coming to my office?"

"We can be there in thirty minutes," Tony answered.

"Alright. I'll see you then," she said. "And I'll start working on the search warrants now."

"Let's go, partner," Tony shouted to Van. He grabbed the homicide folder and they left immediately for the U.S. Attorney's office.

When they arrived, U.S. Attorney Berry introduced them to several other people sitting in the discussion room.

"I'll just go around the table so we're all acquainted. Investigator, Vinnie Morg," she announced, and continued around the table, pointing to each person she named. "Brad Yoraum with the Treasury Department. And TACT Sergeant Justin Nales with the tactical assault crime team. And," she paused, now speaking to the men at the table and gesturing towards Tony and Van, "these two gentlemen are the reason we're here. This is Detective Tony Richards and Detective Van Morris with the homicide squad from the Bronx."

The men all exchanged handshakes and head nods and Tony and Van each took a seat at the table.

"Investigator Morg," Ms. Berry announced, "you have the floor."

"Thanks, Ayesha," he said. "The first thing I want you guys to know is that our investigation started the first day you spoke with Ayesha. We have the records of Ricardo Green's arrests and the history of his life. We also have the purchases that he's made as far back as we could go. We have his current address, a Saint Nicholas Avenue brownstone that he bought cash. Bought his motorcycle and gold Benz with cash as well. He's officially unemployed and has a large sum of money in his mom's name at two separate banks totaling two million dollars. His mom, Elaine Green, still lives at thirty-two twenty-five Eighth, and we have her background as well. I'll pass the floor over to IRS agent, Brad Yoraum."

"Good morning," Mr. Yoraum began. "I have some additional solid info on Ricardo Green. He has never filed income tax, so we can arrest him for tax evasion. And since his bank account is in his mother's name, we can arrest her for undeclared funds. When we execute the search warrant, if there's any more money, we can confiscate that as proceeds from ill-gotten gains. TACT Sergeant, Justin Nales, what have you got?"

"Good morning," Sergeant Nales said. "We contacted the Con Ed Building for floor plans of Greens residence. We've also gotten floor plans from the Housing Authority of apartments eleven A, two A, and four C. We've got photos of Jason Rite and Zak Black at those apartments and upon executing the search and arrest warrants, which we've already obtained, we'll confiscate any evidence. We can discuss times, but in my experience, it'd be best if executed around four a.m. We have undercover vans that hold six men, and we'll need the names of all personnel you want assigned to this case. Me and my men will conduct the breach, and after we call *cleared*, you and your guys can go in and conduct your business. Any questions, suggestions, thoughts?"

"I don't think so," Tony replied. "You guys have it covered. I don't have anything to add. You, Van?"

"No," Van answered. "All sounds good to me."

"We'll get those names for you right away," Tony assured the group.

Ms. Berry treated the group to a working lunch, and Tony and Van gave everyone the information they needed. They agreed to meet her the next day and thanked everyone for all their hard work before they left the office.

"We just gotta follow the money," Tony said to Van as they exited the building.

"I think you're right," Van agreed, and they got in the car to head back to the house.

When they got there, they first met with Sergeant Blackwell and debriefed him on the plan. They confirmed that Detectives Bradberry and Ragland, Jace Ragg, Kenny Land, Cory Anthony, Rock Flow, and Reeshema Porter would be assigned to assist with the warrant, and called all of them into a meeting inside the homicide squad office.

"Alright," Tony started. "The reason we're meeting is because we've made an arrest for the homicide of Carl White. Pursuant to that homicide, we now have cause and reason to make an arrest in Harlem of a big-time drug dealer by the name of Bulldog. We'll be executing arrest and search warrants tomorrow at four a.m. Anyone have a conflict with that so far?"

No one in the room indicated any conflict, so Tony continued.

"We believe that Bulldog will be home, and that the other two crew members will be home also. We're working with the U.S. Attorney's office and anything seized will belong to them. We're just there to assist. However, anything regarding the arrest of Bulldog will go through us. Everybody got that so far?"

Everyone nodded in understanding, so Tony issued individual assignments. He explained that he and Van would be together at Bulldog's house, with Sergeant Blackwell and Detective Porter. Detectives Bradberry, Ragg, and Anthony would go to Jason "Seven" Rite's home. Detectives Ragland, Land, and Flow were assigned to the residence of Zak "Kool" Black's home.

"The U.S. Attorney has a TACT Unit, which is their equivalent to our Emergency Services Unit," Tony explained. "They will breach the doors of all apartments, and we wait until they say *clear* before we go in. Remember, anything found of an evidentiary nature will be turned over to the U.S. Attorney's office. Any questions, suggestions, comments?"

They discussed a few minor details of the plan, but with everyone in accordance, they quickly called it a day.

Chapter 18

At 2:30 a.m., Tony was the first to arrive at the office. He sat down at his desk and went over the TACT plan. Just as he finished reviewing all of the assignments, Van walked in.

"Everything looking good?" Van asked.

"Hey Van," Tony greeted him. "Yeah. I think we're ready."

Everyone drifted in over the next twenty minutes and by five minutes to three, the whole squad was there and raring to go.

"Okay, guys," Tony said. "Be careful today. Keep your heads down and may God bless us." They left the office and met up with the rest of the team at Yankee stadium so they could take the 161st Street Bridge across. They discussed the plan again for about ten minutes then headed up towards the bridge.

Tony rode with Van, Sergeant Blackwell, and Detective Reeshema Porter, and they pulled up in the TACT van right in front of Bulldog's residence. They took a few silent moments to collect themselves, then all officers exited their vans and made their assault.

Tony and his crew waited outside while Sergeant Nales and six of his men, each holding M5 assault rifles, first knocked on the door. Seconds after knocking, they rammed the door and shouted, "U.S. officers! We have a warrant." After receiving no response, the officers forced entry into the building. For what felt like forever, Tony and his team waited outside.

Every sound of the city seemed amplified while they waited, but after just a few minutes, Sergeant Nales called out, "Clear!" On this signal, Tony, Van, Detective Porter, Sergeant Blackwell, Investigator Morg, and the U.S. Attorney entered the building.

It was fabulous. Massive art pieces adorned the walls of the foyer, including a life-sized oil painting of Bulldog holding a bulldog wearing gold chains. A leopard skin upholstered sofa rested on a huge Persian area rug in the room just beyond the entry, and a television the size of a movie theater screen was mounted on the wall opposite the sofa. A glass chandelier with crystal charms and gold and diamond accents hung from the ceiling. By any standards, this was an elaborate and luxurious home.

"Up here, on the second floor," Sergeant Nales shouted.

As he walked up the marble staircase, Tony took note of pictures of Bulldog and his crew on the walls. There were childhood and teenage pictures of all of them, and Tony couldn't help but notice the contrast between the homes and neighborhoods in those pictures and the home in which those pictures were hanging now. On the landing at the top of the stairs was an elaborately framed picture of just Bulldog, holding a gold nine-millimeter handgun, and standing on a bed covered with cash.

Sergeant Nales was standing in the doorway of what seemed to be Bulldog's bedroom. Tony, Van, and Sergeant Blackwell entered the bedroom and saw Bulldog sitting on the floor with his head down and his hands cuffed behind his back. His wife, Zoe, sat next to him in the same exact position. U.S. Attorney Ayesha Berry entered last.

"I'm U.S. Attorney Ayesha Berry," she introduced herself to the couple. "You're being charged with murder one, racketeering, possession of a weapon, and tax evasion."

Bulldog shook his head with a defiant grin and lifted his chin. "Babe, don't say anything to them," he ordered. "I've got the best lawyer money can buy. Just don't say a word."

"That's fine," Ms. Berry said. "You don't have to speak. In fact," she said, laughing ever so slightly, "I suggest you don't. Not until you've had a chance to speak with your attorney. But by law, I have to tell you why you're being arrested." She made eye contact with Sergeant Nales and nodded towards the door. "You can remove him to the Federal facility, along with his wife."

Sergeant Nales then had four of his guys escort them out of the house. After they were gone, Van said, "Can you believe how these people are living? This place should be in a magazine. I've never seen anything like this."

"Neither have I, partner," Tony agreed as he ran his hand along the fur upholstery of a bench beside the bed.

"I'm done here," said Ms. Berry. "You can handle this, right, Detective?"

"Yeah, I got this," Tony replied, and she, Investigator Morg, and the TACT Sergeant and his unit packed up and left the building.

"I'll get patrol to send over a unit to safeguard the building when we're gone," Sergeant Blackwell offered. "Unless you don't need that."

"Eh," Tony shrugged. "Have 'em send over the unit anyway, but I don't care who comes in here when we're gone. We'll just use the unit for crowd control. But we can leave the door wide open for any friendly neighbors in need of free furniture."

"Free furniture?" Van asked in mock excitement. "I gotta go call my wife and get her over here. I need a couple things from this crib at my place."

They all laughed as Van mimed sliding things into his coat pockets. When he opened the night table drawer, he stopped abruptly.

"Bingo!" he exclaimed, not joking this time. He reached into the drawer and pulled out an object wrapped in a gray cloth. "The gold gun."

"Wow," Tony said. "Bold. You would think he woulda gotten rid of that. Then again, he never expected to see us here, did he?"

The search continued for a while. Tony found a safe on the floor in the closet, and called for a hand truck to get it moved. He and Van cleared Bulldog's bedroom while Sergeant Blackwell and Detective Deriggs did the same for the other two bedrooms. From there they moved downstairs to the living room.

Tony and Van searched the kitchen cabinets, the pantry, the refrigerator, and the stove. As they were finishing up, Detective Porter walked in.

"Hey, you guys notice this?" she asked, looking down at the parquet floors. She knelt down to take a closer look at a particular spot near the edge of the cabinet, and then stood up and stomped on it.

Tony and Van watched as she took out her baton and started tapping it on several different areas of the kitchen floor. She tapped again on the same area she had stomped on, making a distinctly different sound from the rest of the floor. She put her baton back in its holster and asked Van to pass her a butter knife from the sink. Using the knife as a lever, Detective Porter slid it between two adjoining wood plates and lifted each of them up.

"Bingo," she said, winking at Van. Underneath the floorboards were four keys of what looked like cocaine.

"I knew I wanted to take you along for something, Reeshema," Tony said, smiling.

"Yeah," Van agreed. "You can come along with us anytime!"

"Just lucky I guess," Detective Porter said. "Working narcotics all these years does pay off."

"You better believe it," Tony replied.

"In all my years, I have never seen this much product from one warrant," said Sergeant Blackwell.

Two police officers entered the living room. "Somebody call for a hand truck?" one of them asked.

"Yeah," Tony answered. "There's a safe upstairs in the closet. Can you guys bring it down and put it in the trunk of the car out front?"

They came down with the safe a few minutes later and Sergeant Blackwell said, "I think that's it, detectives. What else do you need?"

"I think we're done here," Tony sighed. "Let's wrap this up and get downtown to the U.S. Attorney's office."

Chapter 19

When they arrived at the federal building, they removed all the confiscated property from the vehicle. They asked for the property room and then called U.S. Attorney Berry. Ten minutes later, Detectives Ragland and Bradberry showed up with their property.

"Hey guys," said Detective Ragland. "What's up?"

"Hey, Dee," Tony replied. "Kay, how did you guys make out?"

"We each did good," Detective Bradberry replied. "I got a handgun and twenty tin foils of coke. It's a three eighty. He got a handgun – another three eighty – and ten foils of coke."

"Did these guys get their guns at wholesale or something?" Van kidded. "Everybody but the boss has a three eighty."

"What did you guys get?" asked Detective Bradberry.

"We got a safe with unknown contents, a gold nine millimeter – possibly the murder weapon. And four keys of coke, thanks to Reeshema's quick thinking. Did either of your perps say anything?" Tony asked.

"Nothing at all," said Detective Bradberry.

"I expected that," Tony said, nodding. "They've been around the block more than once."

U.S. Attorney Ayesha Berry came into the room. "Hello everyone," she greeted them. "Glad to see that everyone's doing fine. How did your warrants go?"

"Fine," Detective Bradberry answered. "We got several tins foils of coke each and two hand guns."

"Very good," Ms. Berry said. "No problems with the perps?"

"No problems at all," replied Detective Ragland, "other than refusing to give us their names."

Tony and Van shared what they had found, and Ms. Berry agreed to get them help with all of the paperwork they would need to process as well as with opening the safe. They got started on their paperwork as soon as she left the office.

A locksmith showed up just a few minutes later, and in three minutes, he had the safe open. Tony leaned over to look inside. "Looks like I've got some more vouchering to do," he said.

He stood up and stepped aside to reveal four cases of ammunition, two large log books with countless handwritten notations, and what looked like about one hundred thousand dollars in cash. Tony removed it all and placed the contents of the safe on the table.

Two hours later, Tony and Van looked over their completed paperwork and walked over to the processing area. They ran into U.S. Attorney Berry and she invited them to walk with her back to her office.

"I just spoke to Ms. Rachel Simone, the attorney for Mr. Ricardo Green," she explained as she unlocked the door to her office. "Ms. Simone plans to be here in ten minutes. I want you to be here when she arrives, and join us for the conversation."

They reviewed some details of the case until Ms. Berry's secretary called to share that Bulldog's attorney had arrived.

"Send her in," Ms. Berry instructed.

Less than a minute later, a small, red-headed woman in a dark gray suit appeared in the doorway holding a burgundy leather briefcase. She wasn't smiling.

"Hello," Ms. Berry greeted her. "I'm U.S. Attorney Ayesha Berry, and this is Detective Tony Richards and his partner, Detective Van Morris."

"How are you?" the woman said, nodding at and making eye contact with each person in the room. "I'm Rachel Simone, counsel for Mr. Ricardo Green."

Tony and Van stood up and shook hands with the counselor.

"Please, have a seat," said Ms. Berry, motioning towards a chair. "What can I do for you?"

"My client is concerned about the charges," she stated very matter-of-factly. "Can you please tell me what they are?"

"Certainly," Ms. Berry agreed, and she pulled out a piece of paper. "Murder one times five, possession of a weapon, unlawfully discharging a weapon within city limits, possession with the intent to sell narcotics, sale of narcotics, tax evasion, and racketeering."

"I think you forgot to include spitting unlawfully in a public place," Ms. Simone snidely added.

"You know, I did forget about that, didn't I?" Ms. Berry retorted. "I'll be sure to add that as another charge. Does he plan on confessing to that as well?"

"As well? As far as I know, Mr. Green doesn't plan on confessing to anything."

"Well, that's a shame for him because the best thing he can do in his situation is confess. If we have to go to trial, I believe he could get the electric chair."

"Realistically," Ms. Simone said in a condescending tone, "when was the last time anyone actually got the chair?"

"Perhaps he'll just die in jail then," Ms. Berry replied bitingly. "Because he would never get out. Is that why you're here? To discuss his staying in jail the rest of his life?"

"No," she answered firmly. "I'm here to see if we can come to some type of an agreement about the charges Mr. Green is facing."

"We don't plea bargain at the U.S. Attorney's office," Ms. Berry said. "The time that he gets is the time that he gets."

"How much time is he looking at?"

"One hundred ninety-two years."

"One hundred ninety-two years?"

"Still think he won't confess?"

Bulldog's attorney looked out the window without responding for several long, uncomfortable moments. Tony coughed, breaking the silence, and Ms. Simone flashed him a look of defiance before returning her focus to the U.S. Attorney. "And if he confesses?"

"That's another story," Ms. Berry replied. "If he confesses and helps us get someone bigger than him, then we might be able to work something out. It all depends on who and what he gives me. I'm not saying he'll walk free, but maybe he can eventually get out of jail and have some remnant of a life left in the witness protection program."

"Thank you so much for your time," said Ms. Simone, half-heartedly, rising from her seat. "I'll pass this on to Mr. Green and he'll call you with his decision."

"Thank you, Ms. Simone, for coming into my office today," Ms. Berry said. "It's been a real experience talking to you about Mr. Green. Have a good day, now."

"And you," Ms. Simone uttered, head tilted, and she walked out without so much as a glance at Tony or Van.

"You handled her quite well," Tony said, grinning as he stretched his arms in his chair. "I'm impressed."

"So am I!" echoed Van.

"Thanks guys," Ms. Berry answered coyly. "You know a woman's got to do what a woman's got to do."

"You think he's gonna bite?" Tony asked.

"He'd be a fool not to. He better jump at the chance of getting out of jail sometime in this life. I gotta go down to the tombs to talk to him now. Why don't you guys join me?"

"Sounds good," Tony answered, and they went with her to the tombs.

They had to check their guns and batons in the lockers before they could move into the area with the holding cells. Tony and Van followed the U.S. Attorney into Bulldog's cell, and Tony sat directly across from Bulldog and Ms. Simone.

"Hello, I'm U.S. Attorney Ayesha Berry," she introduced herself to Bulldog. "This is the arresting officer, Detective Tony Richards, and sitting behind us is his partner, Detective Van Morris. I've already met with your attorney here, Ms. Simone."

"So, you're the one who got me in this mess?" asked Bulldog defiantly.

"No, you got yourself into this mess," Ms. Berry asserted. "I am the one that's gonna try to help you get yourself out of this mess if you agree to help us." Bulldog smirked and shook his head. Ms. Berry smiled right back. "So, what have you and your attorney decided to do with your life? Are you willing to help yourself?"

"Do you have any witnesses? Or you just bluffing?"

"I don't bluff. I don't play games. I'm just here to find out if you've chosen to confess or not. It's your call."

"If I confess, what can you do for me?"

"Depends on how much you're willing to share. I might be able to knock off some time. Or," Ms. Berry said, no longer smiling, "I could charge your wife with cohesion and charge your mother with tax evasion, since she can't account for the two million dollars in bank accounts under her name. Again, it's your call."

"If I cooperate and give you everything I know, will you let my wife and my mom go?"

"You have my word on that."

"Then let's make a deal," Bulldog conceded.

The U.S. Attorney shook hands with Bulldog, and they all left the room.

"That went well," Van commented as they retrieved their property and headed to the lobby.

"Very well," Tony agreed. "Time will tell, but it does look good."

"Gentlemen, it has been my extreme pleasure to have met and worked with you guys," Ms. Berry said. "I do believe you are the best pair of detectives I've ever worked with. And I mean that."

"Well, this is our first time dealing with the U.S. Attorney's office and I have been impressed since the first day we spoke on the phone," Tony said. "It has been a pleasure for us as well."

"Ditto that," Van added, and Ms. Berry extended her hand.

"We deserve more than a handshake," Tony said, acting offended. "We want a hug." He and Van both hugged the U.S. Attorney and then parted ways with her and headed back to the house.

When they pulled in to the parking lot, Van said, "Great job, partner. We put this whole caper together pretty quick."

"Yeah, let me just give you a little pat on your back there, buddy," Tony said when he got out of the car. They were both laughing as they walked inside.

Van grabbed a marker from his desk and walked over to the homicide chart. He scrawled *CASE CLOSED BY ARREST* across the Ricardo Green case.

Sergeant Blackwell appeared in the doorway to the office. "Great job guys," he said. "Unfortunately, today's my last day working with you. Your boss'll be back tomorrow."

"Well, it's been a blast working with you, Sergeant," Van said. "Sorry to see you leave."

"I hate to see you leave also," Tony added. "But I will be glad to see Sonia."

"I totally get it," Sergeant Blackwell said. "But it has been my pleasure to have worked with you guys." He saluted them and walked away.

"Good guy," Tony said to Van.

"Yeah, he is," Van agreed, and they sat down to start their paperwork for the night.

Chapter 20

"Who's up?"

Tony and Van looked up from the DD5s they had been working on all morning and saw Detective Sergeant Sonia Richards standing in the doorway. "Hey, Sergeant!" Tony exclaimed.

"Sergeant! How you doin'?" Van asked.

"My two favorite life savers," she said, grinning. "How are you guys?" She let out a heavy breath. "I see you guys solved another homicide case. Good for you."

"We owe that one to you, Sergeant," Tony said.

"Yeah," Van agreed. "You taking that bullet is part of what kept us working so hard to get this guy."

"Alright, alright," she said, shrugging off the credit. "So, you gotta give me the four one one about how you collared Bulldog and shut down Harlem's whole north side cocaine ring. I read the papers, but now I need the truth. So, when you get a chance, stop by my office. Good seeing you guys."

"I'm glad she's back," Tony said as she left the office. And he and Van went back to filling out paperwork.

An hour later, they decided to head over to Detective Sergeant Richards' office to give her all the details of Bulldog's case. As they were sharing the full story, and laughing loud enough to be heard all throughout the office, her phone rang.

"Hello?" she answered. "This is she. Yes, sir. Well, thank you, sir. I sure will." She hung up the phone, folded her arms across her chest, and sat back in her chair. "Well, well. Guess what," she said with her eyebrows raised.

"Okay, I'll bite," Tony kidded. "What?"

"We are getting an award," she said, and then she tilted her head and leaned forward on her desk. "And you two are getting promoted."

"You're kidding, right?" asked Van.

"Not kidding. That was the Chief of Detectives calling about Bulldog's case. Awards and a promotion. He said all three of us will be given a meritorious award for bravery, and that you two will be promoted to Second Grade Detective. Congratulations, guys!"

"Thanks! Wow," Tony said, surprised. "Congrats to you, too, Sergeant."

"Yeah, you definitely deserve that award," Van added.

"The ceremony takes place in a week, so go get your uniforms cleaned."

A week later, the mayor of New York City gave them their awards in a ceremony at City Hall, and the Chief of Detectives promoted both Tony and Van to Second Grade Detective. After the ceremony, Tony, Maddie, Van, and Edith went out to dinner to celebrate at the Central Park Restaurant.

About a year and a half later, Tony got a phone call from U.S. Attorney Ayesha Berry.

"How have you been, Tony?"

"Doing quite well and you?"

"I'm fine, fine. I've got an update on Mr. Bulldog," she replied. "First, let me say again how much my office appreciates all the hard work you and Van did on this case. The world is a safer place because of you."

"Thank you," Tony said. "That means a lot."

"Well, it's the truth. Because of you and your partner, Mr. Jules Brown, a.k.a. Light, got ten years for killing Carl White. We've got his mother in witness protection, and he was very helpful in giving us Bulldog, so we've placed him in protective custody. When he leaves, he'll join his mother and they'll be housed together."

"That sounds great," Tony said. "What about the rest of that crew?"

"Well," she started, "Zak Black, a.k.a. Kool, got twenty years for conspiracy and RICO charges. Jason Rite, a.k.a. Seven, also got twenty for the same charges. And Mr. Bulldog himself got thirty for all the murders, conspiracy, RICO, possession, and tax evasion."

"Thirty?" Tony asked in surprise.

"He gave up the person he was getting his coke from," she explained. "And *that* person was supplying the whole borough with coke. We expect that getting that hook-up will get us deep into the core of this drug cartel so we can really work on shutting it down."

"Wow," said Tony. "You guys are awesome. Good stuff."

"I feel the same about you guys. How is Detective Morris?"

"Doing great," Tony answered. "And he's gonna be real pleased about the report you just gave me."

"Well, I just wanted to thank you guys again for doing such a fine job. And by the way, congratulations on your promotion."

"Thank you," Tony said, and then paused for a moment. "Wait, how did you know we got promoted?"

"Eh," Ms. Berry responded. "I might have put in a call to your chief to tell him that I have never worked with two finer detectives."

"Well, thank you, Ms. Berry," Tony repeated. "It was great working with you as well." As Tony put the receiver down, Van walked into the office. Tony flashed a wide grin at him.

"What are you up to?" Van asked suspiciously.

"Not up to anything. Guess who that was?"

"Got me," Van replied.

"That was U.S. Attorney Ayesha Berry calling with the lowdown about how the Bulldog case played out." Tony shared with Van all the details that Ms. Berry had conveyed. Follow the money, partner!" Van exclaimed. "It always leads you to the source."

***

"Who's up?" Detective Sergeant Richards called out.

"I am," Tony replied. "Whatchyu got?"

Acknowledgments

Most novels are the product of research and experience. This is one such novel and is a fictional portrayal of a real homicide I worked on and solved. The event is real, but the names have been changed to protect the innocent, and I would like to thank every relative and friend whose name appears in this book. I would like to thank my wife, my six children, and my two sons-in-law for inspiring and encouraging me to continue telling my stories. Tony Richards was created and would like to continue solving homicides with your support. Thank you to the readers for purchasing my novels and for your support.

Back page

Tony Richards is an NYC Detective, a title that comes with a reputation for being the best in the world. This case puts that perception to the test. Tony Richards has been assigned a homicide case that presents the potential to take down one of the biggest known drug dealers in Harlem. Follow along with him as he investigates this homicide and *follows the money* to make the arrest.

Butch Robinson, Jr. is a retired NYC Detective who has solved many homicides. He is a 911 responder and a Vietnam veteran. He has a wife and six children. This novel portrays the story of a real homicide that he solved, but the names and locations have been changed to protect the innocent. In his retirement, Butch enjoys reading, writing, and playing and teaching chess.